From the Plantation to the Prison

MERCER
UNIVERSITY PRESS

Endowed by
TOM WATSON BROWN
and
THE WATSON-BROWN FOUNDATION, INC.

From the Plantation to the Prison

African-American Confinement Literature

Edited by

Tara T. Green

MERCER UNIVERSITY PRESS
Macon, Georgia

MUP/H746
ISBN 978-0-88146-090-2

First Edition.

Series
Voices of the African Diaspora
Chester J. Fontenot, editor

Library of Congress Cataloging-in-Publication Data

From the plantation to the prison : African-American confinement
literature
/ edited by Tara T. Green. -- 1st ed.
p. cm.
Includes bibliographical references and index.
ISBN-13: 978-0-88146-090-2 (hardback : alk. paper)
ISBN-10: 0-88146-090-7 (hardback : alk. paper)
1. American literature—African American authors—History and criticism.
2. African Americans—Intellectual life. 3. African Americans in literature.
4. Imprisonment in literature. 5. Prisoners in literature.
I. Green, Tara T.
PS153.N5F76 2008
810.9'3556--dc22
2008006227

Contents

Acknowledgments

This project developed out of a 2002 College Language Association panel where I invited John Lowe of Louisiana State University and Carol E. Henderson of the University of Delaware to present papers on the subject of African-American confinement literature. At that conference I approached Chester Fontenot, Jr., with my idea of developing the panel discussion into a collection of essays on a subject that I felt had not been sufficiently explored. And, through his support as a valued colleague and industrious series editor, the project has become a book.

Through a summer research grant provided by Southern University in 2003, I was able to forgo teaching to review and edit the first drafts of the collection. The grant also funded a trip to the Schomburg Research Center where, with the help of its staff, I was able to learn more about Malcolm X through a review of Alex Haley's papers. Another grant, awarded by Northern Arizona University, allowed me to focus more time on editing the project and doing the research required to develop the introduction.

I am most thankful to all of the contributors without whose dedication to writing and research this collection would not have been possible. Thank you all for enduring with patience.

A book cannot proceed without the invaluable help of persons committed to the editorial process. I am grateful to Louella Holter of Northern Arizona's Bilby Research Center for her help in preparing the manuscript for Mercer University Press.

The inspiration for this project and much of what I do as an African Americanist who was raised in the American South has its roots in my family. From my parents, Delores and Edmond Green, I have come to know about a time that was not mine, but theirs, and to better understand my legacy and purpose in this world. With them, was my late maternal grandmother Isabella Thomas and her children, whose childhood memories of tedious work in cotton fields inform my sense of racial, social, and economic boundaries and the possibilities of moving beyond them.

Bring my soul out of prison, that I may give thanks to thy name: the righteous shall compass me about; for thou shalt deal bountifully with me.

Psalms 142:7

Series Preface

When Tara Green first mentioned her plans to edit a collection of essays on African-American confinement literature, I thought it was a great idea, but was not convinced that she could bring the project to fruition. My caveat had nothing to do with Tara's scholarly promise or editorial skills. Rather, it was the result of my knowledge of the scarceness of scholarship in this subgenre of African-American writing. For most scholars working in the field of African-American literature, confinement or prison writings have been relegated to the less serious genre of popular literature, not worthy of serious scholarly attention.

This perspective toward this body of writing has won the day, for the most part, in spite of the fact that a number of these texts were written by or about significant public figures in the African-American cultural tradition, i.e., Malcolm X, Angela Davis, Eldridge Cleaver, George Jackson, Martin Luther King, etc. When one expands the genre of prison writings to include African Americans writing within the delimited space of confinement, as Tara Green does in this collection, the list of authors subject to critical analysis becomes staggering. For not only does this genre include writings by African Americans who have been physically imprisoned, but also literature written by those who have been or are being confined socially, politically, and economically. For Tara Green, confinement is a trope within the African-American cultural tradition that signifies the way African Americans have been culturally imprisoned, so to speak, within the private spaces of blackness. Defined in this way, African-American confinement literature cuts across other genres and holds the possibility of being a significant signifier of black identity in America and throughout the Diaspora.

I see this book as the beginning of serious scholarly work in a genre that is both new and old, for these writings have been with us for a long time. They have subsisted, so to speak, within the African-American tradition, and most have been ignored by literary critics. It is my hope that this collection will spur others to enter the world of African-American confinement literature and subject these writings to serious scholarly scrutiny.

Chester J. Fontenot, Jr.
Voices of the African Diaspora series editor

Introduction

Tara T. Green

In *Soledad Brother*, George Jackson writes that he was convicted of stealing $70 and sentenced to serve a term of one year to life at the age of eighteen. While at Soledad Prison, he was charged with killing a guard and was forced to endure solitary confinement twenty-three hours per day. Jackson offers that life in America as a black man prepared him for prison existence: "Blackmen born in the U.S. and fortunate enough to live past the age of eighteen are conditioned to accept the inevitability of prison....Being born a slave in a captive society and never experiencing any objective basis for expectation had the effect of preparing me for the progressively traumatic misfortune that led so many blackmen to the prison gate. I was prepared for prison. It required only minor psychic adjustments."[1] Although "the walls of the prison exclude the public from all direct knowledge of what is taking place behind them,"[2] solitary confinement created within Jackson the desire to find his voice through writing. His voice is an expression within the state confinement that challenges the system designed to render prisoners voiceless and powerless. Jackson's reference to the expectation that black men will

---

[1]George Jackson, *Soledad Brother* (New York: Coward McCann and Bantam 1970) 1.

[2]H. Bruce Franklin, introduction to *Prison Writing in the 20th-Century* (New York: Penguin Books 1998) 2.

eventually be imprisoned is similar to other black male prison writers, including Martin Luther King, Jr., Malcolm X, Marcus Garvey, and Frederick Douglass. For example, Malcolm X, compares the prison system to the welfare system that led to the demise of his family's unit. Like Jackson does in *Soledad Brother*, Malcolm X links life as a black American and life as a convicted criminal as inextricably bound when he states "Don't be shocked when I say that I was in prison. You're still in prison. That's what America means: prison."[3] As a statement of fact, his words ring true when applied to the experiences of African Americans. Though Malcolm X is paroled and reaches a level of national notoriety, he never lets black Americans believe that a life outside of bars means that they are free.

Unfortunately, black men are not the only victims of the prison system. Black women have also experienced confinement. One only needs to remember the images of Rosa Parks as she was being booked at the Montgomery, Alabama, jail for violating a bus segregation seating law, or the story of Fannie Lou Hamer,[4] who was beaten and sexually threatened in a Mississippi jail following her arrest for daring to register black voters, or the publicity related to activist and professor Angela Davis who was made famous when she was sought and subsequently arrested for her alleged role in the shooting of a California judge.

Perhaps the beginning of the experiences of people of African descent in the New World established the trope of confinement that we find in the writings of African Americans. Frederick Douglass portrayed the experience of slavery as a

---

[3]George Breitman, ed., *Malcolm Speaks: Selected Speeches and Statements* (New York: Grove Press, 1965) 8.

[4]Bettye Collier-Thomas and V. P. Franklin, *Sisters in the Struggle: African American Women in the Civil Rights-Black Power Movement* (New York: New York University Press, 2001).

"prison-house," an institution that legally restricted slaves from being educated while legally categorizing them as property.[5]

Since 1865 and the passing of the Thirteenth Amendment, the nature of confinement for blacks took other forms. H. Bruce Franklin cites several forms of slavery that were designed to keep people of African descent as laborers, including, among others, work on chain gangs. Perhaps the form that most closely resembled slavery was designating blacks as criminals if they displayed no "visible signs of support," or were found guilty of "loitering" or "vagrancy." Once arrested, they would often become part of the convict lease system that allowed prisons to lease convicts to private contractors for cheap labor.[6] This system was, "worse than slavery" as David M. Oshinsky indicates, since the workers were required to work without any remuneration and under intense conditions.

Given the similarities of experiences from one era to the next, it is more appropriate to describe the experiences of black men and women under slavery, during Reconstruction, and within the penal system as confinement. Since imprisonment refers to a physical state of existence when men and women are sentenced to serve time in an institution because they have committed a crime, the time they serve is thought of as punishment for breaking laws established by the government; it is restitution or penitence. Confinement, on the other hand, describes the status of individuals who are placed within boundaries—either seen or unseen—but always felt. It describes the status of persons who are imprisoned and who are unjustly relegated to a social and political status that is hostile, rendering them powerless and subject to the rules of those who have assumed a position of authority. Confinement, then, appropriately describes the status

---

[5]Frederick Douglass, *Narrative of the Life of Frederick Douglass, An American Slave* (New York: Penguin, 1986) 121.

[6]Franklin, introduction to *Prison Writing*, 4–5.

of African Americans who have endured spaces of confinement that include for example plantations, Jim Crow societies, and prisons. At specific times, these "spaces of confinement" have been used to oppress African Americans socially, politically, and spiritually. Though they may not be prisoners, historically African Americans have been subject to laws that restrict their right to enjoy the rights and privileges that all American citizens are guaranteed by the US Constitution.

The essays in this collection examine a number of texts defined as African-American confinement literature—auto-biographies, essays, novels, and poems—that are set either entirely or partly in a place of confinement, including plantations, prisons, and segregated societies, and tell of African Americans' experiences with incarceration. In response to this literature, the scholars of this collection survey the history of the confinement of African Americans as a physical and sometimes a spiritual state that is sanctioned by federal and state laws.

For the most part, this collection addresses one of the concerns posed by Angela Y. Davis, who observes that black men are the primary targets of the criminal justice system.[7] This book is divided into two parts, and the essays focus primary on black men. Part 1, "Identifying the Boundaries of Confinement," begins with "Writing from No Man's Land: The Black Man's Quest for Freedom from Behind the Walls" by Carol E. Henderson. Henderson uses the personal narratives of incarcerated black men Eldridge Cleaver, Nathan McCall, and Malcolm X to demonstrate how convicted black male writers construct a "speakerly voice" in an effort to transform themselves within "the fixed boundaries of their circumstances." She argues, in essence, that through their prison narratives, they reclaim themselves "through the channels of the mind."

---

[7] Angela Y. Davis. "From the Convict Lease System," in *States of Confinement*, ed. Joy James (New York: St. Martins, 2000) 61.

In her essay, "Lessons before Dying: The Contemporary Confined Character-in-Process," Dana Williams argues that African-American male authors use the trope of confinement to develop their African-American male heroes as characters-in-process. This four-step process includes examination of the self while in confinement, reaffirmation of one's humanity or individuality after confinement, investigation of strategies of survival, and finally attempts to assert the redefined self. She uses the texts of Richard Wright's *Native Son*, Ralph Ellison's *Invisible Man*, Leon Forrest's *The Bloodworth Orphans*, and Ernest Gaines's *A Lesson before Dying* in the analysis.

In conversation with Williams, in his essay "Mind-Blown: Possibility and Trauma in *Native Son*," Terry Bozeman uses Søren Kierkegaard's theory of possibility of understanding the life and actions of Bigger Thomas. Bozeman's goal is to explore the relevance of confinement on the psychological development of Bigger.

Part 2, "Confined Spaces and Places begins with a discussion by Katherine Daley and Carolyn M. Jones in their essay "Ernest Gaines's *A Lesson before Dying*: Freedom in Confined Spaces." They argue that Gaines's novel uses Christian symbols and myths as vehicles for communicating a set of values that Gaines associates with manhood. Spaces of confinement and imprisonment become places of freedom for Grant and Jefferson.

In her essay "Doing Time in/as 'The Monster': Abject Identity in African-American Prison Literature," Kimberly Drake uses the fiction and autobiographical testimony of Chester Himes and other convicted authors, as well as references to the depictions of inmates in the television series *Oz*, to trace how prison experiences replace the individual convict's identity, particularly racial identity, with a uniformed institutional identity. Finally, Jeff Loeb discusses the impact of race on the confinement narratives of black prisoners of war in "Faith's

Fickle Covenant: African-American Captivity Narratives from the Vietnam War."

It is my hope that this collection of essays will open new avenues of inquiry into confinement literature. The Bureau of Justice Department indicates that in 2005 out of every 100,000 Americans, 800 blacks compared to 166 whites are incarcerated.[8] More specifically, "Although black people make up just 12 percent of the population, they make up nearly 44 percent of the prison population."[9] These alarming statistics support the claims of the writers whose texts are discussed herewith that, for black people, life in America is too often a confining experience.

Works Cited

Breitman, George, editor. *Malcolm Speaks: Selected Speeches and Statements*. New York: Grove Press, 1965.

Bureau of Justice. http://www.ojp.usdoj.gov/bjs, 26 August 2006.

Collier-Thomas, Bettye, and V. P. Franklin. *Sisters in the Struggle: African American Women in the Civil Rights-Black Power Movement*. New York: New York University Press, 2001.

Cosby, Bill and Alvin F. Poussaint. *Come on People: On the Path from Victims to Victors*. Nashville: Thomas Nelson, 2007.

Davis, Angela Y. "From the Convict Lease System." In *States of Confinement*, edited by Joy James, 60–74. New York: St. Martins, 2000.

Douglass, Frederick. *Narrative of the Life of Frederick Douglass, An American Slave*. New York: Penguin, 1986.

---

[8] Department of Justice, www.usdoj.gov/ (26 August 2006).

[9] Bill Cosby and Alvin F. Poussaint, *Come on People: On the Path from Victims to Victors* (Nashville: Thomas Nelson, 2007) 9.

Franklin, H. Bruce. *Prison Writing in the 20th Century*. New York: Pcnguin Books, 1998.

Jackson, George. *Soledad Brother*. New York: Coward McCann and Bantam, 1970.

Oshinsky, David M. *"Worse than Slavery": Parchman Farm and the Ordeal of Jim Crow Justice*. New York: Free Press, 1996.

Part I

Identifying the Boundaries of Confinement

Writing from No Man's Land: The Black Man's Quest for Freedom from Behind the Walls

Carol E. Henderson

After I returned to prison, I took a long look at myself and, for the first time in my life, admitted that I was wrong, that I had gone astray—astray not so much from the white man's law as from being human, civilized....My pride as a man dissolved and my whole fragile moral structure seemed to collapse, completely shattered. That is why I started to write. To save myself.[1]

To be or not to be....that is the question.[2]

Originally I had titled this essay "Freedom to Self-Create: Identity and the Politics of Movement in Contemporary Narratives from Prison" because, as Robert Butler argues, "a central quest in American life is for pure motion, movement either for its own sake or as a means of freeing oneself from a prior mode of existence."[3] My intent was to extrapolate upon the

---

[1]Eldridge Cleaver, *Soul on Ice* (New York: Dell Publishing, 1991) 27.
[2]William Shakespeare, *Hamlet*.
[3]Robert Butler, *Contemporary African American Fiction: The Open Journey* (Madison: Fairleigh Dickinson University Press, 1998) 11.

generic version of prison narratives—those accounts steeped in the unbridled legacy of a people seeking to reconstruct a political voice, indeed a personhood from behind the veil of cyclical ignorance and racism that has so infectiously imprisoned African Americans and their social contemporaries in co-dependent relationships. This line of inquiry would have me relegate my discussion of prison narratives to those narratives shaped primarily around the ways of "blackness" and the sociopolitical investments of people like Angela Davis, Rosa Parks, and Martin Luther King, Jr., whose odysseys help shaped the Civil Rights Movement of the 1960s. These narratives stress inclusion in the political and social processes of this country and an acknowledgment of the socially debilitating forces that have literally and figuratively enslaved African Americans in a cultural "wasteland" of inopportunity.

I would, however, like to expand the critical optic of that discussion to include other non-fictional texts that, like their fictional counterparts, seek to reaffirm black citizenry—indeed black personhood—through an examination of the incarcerated black male body. The body—as fleshly and sacred being—has continued to serve as a medium for the conceptualizations of national identities. As sign and symbol, the body's narrative abilities stem from its contentious evolvement as a paradoxical social being, that is, the way the body is identified and contextualized in the social, political, and historical arenas of dominant society that revolve around the pretentious nature of America's body politic. This politic, framed around what Karen Sanchez-Eppler calls "the bodily biases of the state,"[4] creates a political and legal climate that consolidates the privileges of white men through the repetitive *re*invention of those public discourses that shape our understanding of the national subject. Within this

---

[4]Karen Sanchez-Eppler, *Touching Liberty: Abolition, Feminism, and the Politics of the Body* (Berkeley: University of California Press, 1993) 3.

context, the African-American body has been viewed more or less as a composite of social meanings—meanings that, in the end, *mark* this body as "bodiless" according to specific cultural and national mandates that objectify the African-American body so much so that black identity is formed in relation to the split between mind and body. Implicit in this discussion is the struggle for control of the black body—both as a material agent and as a spiritual entity.

It is against this backdrop that authors Nathan McCall (*Makes Me Wanna Holler*) and Eldridge Cleaver (*Soul on Ice*) fashion an autobiographical self in language that not only recoups this body, but also writes into existence the cultural angst and sobering rage that inhabit black men's reality in this country. If, as James Baldwin reminds us, "to be black and conscious in America is to be in a constant state of rage,"[5] then McCall and Cleaver's literary forays into the exigency of a black manhood under siege transforms the fixed boundaries of that subsistence, providing for them an avenue by which they may perform a literary "exorcism" of sorts, a spiritual interrogation of that space Richard Wright calls "No Man's Land." Because the methodological figurings of the systems of oppression consistently silence the voice of the disempowered using the body as its vehicle, these writers must reclaim that body *discursively* in order to facilitate a counter-discourse that *re*conceptualizes the meanings of literal and figurative bodies within certain predetermined social structures. It is the gap between these two categories that allows for the possibility of speaking a counter-discourse of the body—a body disfigured by the toxins of racism.

As Wright states in "How 'Bigger' Was Born," Bigger's existence hovered between two worlds—between powerful

---

[5]Quoted in Joan Didion, *The White Album*, (New York: Simon and Schuster, 1979) 30.

America and his own stunted place in life.[6] Thus as writer, his job was to humanize this space, to make the reader *feel* this place and know the consistency of its boundaries. As Wright concludes, "[the] imaginative novel represents, in a fundamental sense, the merging of two extremes; it is an intensely intimate expression on the part of a consciousness couched in terms of the most objective and commonly known events. It is at once something private and public by its very nature and texture...[and as] a kind of community of exchange, what [is] read, felt, thought, seen, and remembered is translated into extensions"[7] of social materiality that are reworked in the collective un-conscious. Wright's literary exploration of Bigger Thomas's journey to "self" thus affords us an opportunity to finger, as well, the fissures of the black male psyche—a psyche dwarfed in the shadow of a cultural nemesis fed by the distorted longings of a nation. It is in wrestling with this shadowy existence that we see the most stimulating view of personal recreation in verse as the quest for selfhood and dignity becomes the impetus for a restructuring of African-American subjectivity.

This transformation can be clearly traced in Eldridge Cleaver's searing narrative *Soul on Ice*. Hauntingly eloquent in its simplicity, Cleaver's memoirs chart his struggle to chisel away at the calcified remnants of a self disassembled by self-hatred and that hatred directed at him by others. The former minister of information for the Black Panthers, Cleaver penned this series of essays and letters during his nine-year stint in California's tough San Quentin and Folsom Prisons for assault with intent to murder. After his release in 1966, Cleaver helped establish the Black Panthers, a militant, anti-establishment black-nationalist group based in Oakland, California. *Soul on Ice* was published two

---

[6]Richard Wright, "How 'Bigger' Was Born," in *Native Son* (New York: HarperPerennial, 1998) 451.
[7]Ibid., 433.

years later and became not only an American classic, but also the philosophical foundation of the Black Power movement, as one critic put it.[8] Cleaver's work is a product of a decade filled with protest and anger, rebellion and revolution. The cover of *Soul on Ice* speaks to Cleaver's condition, as does the title of the book—it features an image of his rugged face and unkempt hair juxtaposed with that of a block of ice imprinted with the frozen and unknown images of other men. Like the prison block that houses him, Cleaver's soul is "on ice"—an allegory of the experiences of thousands of young men who languish in prison—exiled from their own communities *in* their own country. As Ishmael Reed concludes in the preface to the book, "Had Cleaver remained in prison...he'd probably be dead."[9] Thus writing became life itself, a way of becoming for Cleaver that signified, on a larger scale, the journeys of every man—poor, black, and disenfranchised in the land of plenty.

Cleaver's exposé of life "behind the wall" is brutally honest yet remarkable in revealing his process of self-analysis, self-expression, and self-education. Often these examinations lay bare the *rituals* of law enforcement as the body of the condemned is fractured through a discourse of punishment that separates the dis-eased body from society, and in the interim, disconnects the individual from himself. Cleaver's forays into the *process* of self-discovery and self-affirmation are reminiscent of Etheridge Knight's explorations of self in his volume *Poems from Prison*, particularly his elegy "The Idea of Ancestry." In this lament, he declares that his experiences in isolation put him in touch with those selves mirrored in the faces of the forty-seven family members taped to the wall of his cell, those selves creatively tied to the graves of his grandfathers and "the brown hills and red

---

[8]Jennifer Auther et al., "'He Was a Symbol': Eldridge Cleaver Dies at 62," *CNN News*, www.cnn.com/US/9805/01/cleaver.late.obit (1 May 1998) 2.
[9]Ishmael Reed, preface, *Soul on Ice*, xvii.

gullies of Mississippi."[10] Knight's inability to fully return to that place of his ancestry, "like a salmon quitting the cold ocean-leaping and bucking up his birthstream" stems from the "gray stone wall damming [his] stream."[11] This wall, emblematic of his incarceration and the demons of his past, anchors Knight's spiritual self to the physical jail cell he inhabits. Knight's way around this wall, both literally and figuratively, is to tap into those communal and spiritual ties that allow him to reconcile his past in a manner that moves him beyond his present to a future of alternative possibilities. "I am all of them, they are all of me," Knight writes, focusing his reader on those aspects of his identity that are a paradoxical mixture of cultural and spiritual energy.[12]

Knight's reflections direct attention to his process of being—a journey intimately tied to his quest for autonomy and self-governing. It is in this borderland of naming and self-discovery that Knight and Cleaver "call and respond" to the shared pain of personal and familial isolation. "I used to lie awake at night racked by painful craving to take a leisurely stroll under the stars, or to go to the beach, to drive a car on a freeway, to grow a beard, or to make love to a woman.... I suffered," writes Cleaver.[13] This bodily affliction amplifies the spiritual absence of creative human connection, which "is not nourished in prison."[14] Cleaver realizes that "no one could save me but myself."[15] Thus begins his odyssey to personal rediscovery.

Knight's (and likewise Cleaver's) self-reflexive postures in their writings provide ample evidence of the assertions of

---

[10]Etheridge Knight, "The Idea of Ancestry," in *Norton Anthology of African American Literature*, ed. Henry Louis Gates, Jr., and Nellie Y. McKay (New York: W. W. Norton, 1997) 1867.

[11]Ibid.

[12]Ibid.

[13]Cleaver, *Soul on Ice*, 20.

[14]Ibid., 28.

[15]Ibid., 27.

imaginative movement as these call into question not only the ambiguous forms of historical, social, and political silencing that impinge upon the fundamental liberties of a people in search of space to breathe; these artistic posturings also bring to bear the radical forms of social injustice that stifle spiritual growth. This practice concretizes the pathological nature of penalization as the enclosed, segmented space of the cell produces an alternative city whose inhabitants are reminded day after day of their internal as well as their physical exile. Cleaver's chapters that explore the prison world, particularly "A Day in Folsom Prison," describe with keen acuity the daily exercise of the body—from morning calisthenics to evening bouts with a punching bag, a basketball, or a handball. Such activities were far and few between, as Cleaver discloses that he spent on average a total of seventeen hours a day in his cell. This isolation leads to a systematic dismantling of his psyche. To combat this malaise, Cleaver begins to read and write. He is desperate to "seek the light" in books that speak of his lived experience as a black man. His personal writings represent a conscious effort to *see* a true self as he reassembles the fragments of a dispossessed and tortured being. As Cleaver explains, his pride as a man had dissolved and his fragile moral structure had collapsed upon his reentry into prison—"the price of hating other human beings," he writes. "I started to write to save myself.... The prison authorities were both uninterested and unable to help me. I had to seek out the truth and unravel the snarled web of my motivations."[16] This journey leads him to realistically assess who he has become and where he has arrived as an evolved being: "I am perfectly aware that I'm in prison, that I'm a Negro, that I've been a rapist, and that I have a Higher Uneducation. I never know what significance I'm supposed to attach to these factors."[17]

---

[16]Ibid.
[17]Ibid., 30.

But the informed reader knows what meanings to ascribe to these signifiers for when taken as whole, these labels represent a stream of perpetual prisons—interlocutory systems that detail the ways in which the black male body is marked—bound mind, body, and spirit—by institutionalized oppression. Cleaver's redemption then rests not only on his own acknowledgment of his physical and spiritual exile, but on our recognition of his becoming something else, an *ideal* of his former self that has shed the clothing of these previous markers to arrive at a more substantive space from which to speak. Cleaver is not always successful in his attempts to recreate himself, for as he readily admits, "In Richard Wright's *Native Son*, I found Bigger Thomas and a keen insight into the problem."[18] Because Wright's Bigger remains a modern codification of black manhood stunted by his literal and discursive cages, Cleaver's struggle centers on finding a language through these walls that will allow him to engage in a spirited interrogation of black masculinity that explores the twisted chronological context of this complicated history as he simultaneously lays bare his own complicity in his alienation.

It is significant that much of *Soul on Ice* defines the various prisms that young black men find themselves in—prisms that, in the end, reveal the intimate connection between the spiritual strivings of a people and the bitter reality of life in America. From his reflections on the images of the black eunuch to his critical rendering of the portrait of the super masculine menials,[19] Cleaver allegorizes black life through his discussion of the class society—a society alienated by an eternal struggle between the haves and the have nots. Cleaver's attention to the emasculative practices of segregation (be they economic, political, or otherwise) and the moral disassembling of the black male psyche points up the ways in which black men seek to

---

[18]Ibid., 23.
[19]See section four of Cleaver's *Soul on Ice*, particularly pages 145 and 168.

lessen the spiritual hemorrhaging of their communities by transforming the socially accepted self-image of Uncle Tom into a cultural Lazarus with the spirit of John Henry.

> The New Testament parable of Jesus raising Lazarus from the dead is interpreted by the Black Muslims as a symbolic parallel to the history of the Negro in America. By capturing black men in Africa and bringing them to slavery in America, the white devils *killed* the black man...transforming him into a "Negro," the symbolic Lazarus left in the "graveyard" of segregation and second-class citizenship. And just as Jesus was summoned to the cave to raise Lazarus from the dead, Elijah Muhammad had been summoned by God to lift up the modern Lazarus, the Negro, from his grave.[20]

Elijah Muhammad's role as savior in this illustration is significant in understanding the degree to which certain images of black masculinity are buried and then resurrected through certain religious practices as well as a number of other venues such as music and sports.[21] Cleaver, in particular, cites the sport of boxing as "the two-fisted testing ground of manhood."[22] The champion in this sport is not only viewed as a symbol of America; he is the embodiment of the Darwinian ritual of the survival of the fittest—the personification of myth and subliminal suggestion. As the "ultimate focus of masculinity in America," boxing manifests itself as a perverse national pastime that not only "reveals us as a nation of peep freaks" but also demonstrates

---

[20]Cleaver, *Soul on Ice*, 94.

[21]The importance of Elijah Muhammad's role in reframing the discussion of black masculinity requires more room to discuss than I have here. What I can say is that Muhammad's philosophical tenets concerning naming are crucial to severing the ties to a slave historicity invented in America.

[22]Cleaver, *Soul on Ice*, 85.

"the insatiable appetite of the de facto jungle law underlying our culture."[23] Under this guise, boxing transports its fighter and spectator into the unbridled conundrum of symbolic victory—a victory that can become a counterrevolutionary act, according to Cleaver.[24] Thus what is at stake is the ability to recreate one's self—the ability to reconstitute one's personage and that of one's community. In commenting on the Muhammad Ali–Floyd Patterson fight, Cleaver writes: "The fight was ideological, a pivotal event, reflecting the consolidation of certain psychic gains of the Negro revolution....Both black and white America, looking on, were sucked into the vortex of the event, feeling somehow a profound relationship to what was being enacted in that ring. They knew that a triumph and a defeat were taking place with consequences for America, transcending the fortunes of the men squaring off in the ring to test their strength."[25] As a result, boxing becomes a war of wills that centers around race and its inevitable ties to that body buried in the symbolic crypts of black subjugation. In returning to the biblical parable of Lazarus, Cleaver draws parallels between this body and that reinvented black body resurrected in the ring through victory. In his analysis of Lazarus/Ali and Jesus/Elijah Muhammad, Cleaver distinguishes between the character difference between that "Lazarus-man created in the crucible of hatred and pain" and the Lazarus-man confined to the psychic mechanism of white America: "Cassius Clay, shedding his graveyard identity like an old dead skin, is one who heeded Elijah's call, repudiating the identity America gave him and taking on a new identity—Muhammad Ali. Floyd Patterson did not heed Elijah."[26] Thus Patterson's defeat was viewed as a victory for the new Lazarus-man because in defeating

---

[23]Ibid.
[24]Ibid., 91.
[25]Ibid.
[26]Ibid., 94 and 91 respectively.

Patterson, the "bootlicking art of the puppet in the style of his image" was defeated in hand-to-hand combat, reminiscent of the way in which Frederick Douglass frees himself from the clutches of slavery during his physical confrontation with the overseer Edward Covey.[27] Moreover, the transformations echoed in both the Cleaver and Douglass narratives join an interesting thread of personal restoration that bears witness to the persistent need to acquire voice through writing in a way that liberates the spirit and frees the soul.

Cleaver's narrative mirrors the national and political concerns of a generation embroiled in the clutches of segregation. Nathan McCall's *Makes Me Wanna Holler* (1994) extends Cleaver's examination, in some respects, by focusing on the nationalist tendencies that point up the blatant and subtle forms of racism that fuel America's "UnderEducation."[28] A *Washington Post* reporter, McCall's autobiography chronicles his journey from the street to the prison yard, and eventually to the newsroom where he distinguished himself as a respected journalist. McCall's spiritual odyssey from prison to college reinvokes the cultural memory of a long line of literary godfathers whose journeys through the virtual prison systems of our society gave birth to a new process of being for most African-American men. As critic William Lyne reminds us, McCall's "early life of racial hardship, criminality, drugs, and prison...joins the tradition of literary realism that runs from Frederick Douglass to hip-hop."[29] This literary aesthetic of conversion and redemption is a staple in autobiographical texts written by men of color, but their critical

---

[27]See Frederick Douglass's *Narrative of the Life of Frederick Douglass, an American Slave* (1845; reprint, New York: W. W. Norton and Company, 1997) chap. 10, specifically pp. 49 and 50.

[28]Here I am borrowing Cleaver's use of the term in his autobiography *Soul on Ice* (30).

[29]William Lyne, "No Accident: From Black Power to Black Box Office," *African American Review* 34/1 (Spring 2000): 45.

purpose is undervalued in mainstream America due to the fundamental oversight of literary and cultural traditions that classify these narratives as something other than political expression. This strategy separates these texts from more mainstream liberal approaches to political dissent and leads to a misrepresentation of the black autobiographical voice. As a result, "black cultural nationalism becomes the necessary, easily demonized and contained Other that gives the illusion of oppositional space, while Black dissent that moves away from race and toward class and economics is excluded from the conversation."[30] Lyne's observations are key to understanding the body politics of Cleaver and McCall, as their narratives seek to speak transformation to the black underclass that languishes in the margins of American society unheard. By deeming their own incarcerated bodies viable, Cleaver and McCall begin the process of empowerment as they discursively reclaim a black body voided by the body politic.

Critic Gail Jardine was correct when she argued that McCall's autobiographical unfolding of his past "evokes the tremors of many American transformative accounts, and his work stands as a reminder that transformation undergirds the American experience."[31] Specifically, McCall's narrative calls forth and extends the conversionary exploits of one African-American leader, Malcolm X, whose ascent from street hustler to international world leader stands as one of the most astounding testaments to the spirit. Malcolm's *Autobiography* is a veritable history, "a series of incarnations," borrowing Joseph Henry's phrase,[32] of the process of becoming a man who, in the personage of Malcolm

---

[30]Ibid.

[31]Gail Jardine, "To Be Black, Male, and Conscious: Race, Rage, and Manhood in America," *American Quarterly* 48/2 (June 1996): 385.

[32]Joseph Henry, "The Public, Spiritual, and Humanistic Odyssey of Malcolm X: A Critical Bibliographical Debate," *Iowa Journal of Literary Studies* 4/1 (1983): 78.

Little, experienced the nightmare of racism.[33] His psychical
journey through his various personas—Malcolm Little, Detroit
Red, Satan, Minister Malcolm X, and finally, El-Hajj Malik El-
Shabazz—represents, in many ways, his valiant attempts to
grapple with the reality of a black manhood birthed in the
crucible of anguish and detestation. It is his stint as Satan,
though, that ties him to the cyclical nature of self-hatred and
violence. As Joseph Henry aptly observes, angry stalking in
prison earned Malcolm the identity of the ultimate outlaw, Satan,
"revealing a spiritual state of mind even beyond atheism."[34]
Critic Sidonie Smith puts it another way: Malcolm's "physical
imprisonment is the literal equivalent of his spiritual
imprisonment," and this condition is "symbolic of the bars that
the black American faces all his life as a second-class citizen."[35]
Henry and Smith's assessments certainly bring to bear the
precarious intellectual and emotional tightrope African-American
men must walk in order to master any semblance of spiritual or
cultural wholeness. In reflecting on Malcolm's journey (and
summarily McCall's evolution from prison to college)—each
man's sojourn through the developmental vortex of racialized
America *is* every black man's journey from slavery to freedom
despite the historical curse of death so prevalent in their lives.

That is why Malcolm's autobiography is regarded as a
classic—not only amongst prison inmates, but also within the
general population of black men as a whole. As Nate McCall

---

[33]As is common knowledge (and is also stated in *The Autobiography of
Malcolm X*), Malcolm experienced the death of his father who, as a
revolutionary, was murdered by the Klan in a most violent way: a train beheaded
him after he was tied to the railroad tracks near his home. This patriarchal void
created a monumental obstacle in Malcolm's identity formation, which he
"acted out" through crime and substance abuse before his transformation in
prison through the teachings of the Nation of Islam.

[34]Henry, "Odyssey of Malcolm X," 80–81.

[35]Sidonie Smith, *Where I'm Bound: Patterns of Slavery and Freedom in Black
American Autobiography* (Westport CT: Greenwood Press, 1974) 153.

himself states, "Malcolm's tale helped me understand the devastating effects of self-hatred and introduced me to a universal principle: that if you change your self-perception, you can change your behavior."[36] Thus Malcolm's autobiography is considered a venerable passageway to the transformation of spirit and mind, and the literary responses to his life become figurative replications of this process. For this reason, X's narrative has a particular resonance among individuals systematically tied to the penal industry. "Malcolm X had a special meaning for black convicts," Eldridge Cleaver explains. "A former prisoner himself, he had risen from the lowest depths to the greatest heights...he was a symbol of hope, a model for thousands of black convicts who found themselves trapped in the vicious PPP cycle: prison-parole-prison."[37] McCall echoes this sentiment in his text: "every chance I got, [I was] trying to more fully understand why my life and the lives of friends had been so contained and predictable, and why prison—literally—had become a rite of passage for so many of us."[38]

McCall's literary indictment of the perils of black male existence in the age of promise is particularly troubling as the political and social gains made during the Civil Rights Movement of the 1960s seem to dissipate under the harsh realities of urbanization and economic segmentation. McCall's dissent into criminal life comes as a result of black rage, that unbridled emotion folded into violence and hate that stems from the knowledge of knowing he *is* a "soul on ice": "Sometimes, when I sit back and think about the crazy things the fellas and I did and remember the hate and violence that we unleashed, it's hard to believe I was once part of all that—I feel so removed from it now

---

[36]Nathan McCall, *Makes Me Wanna Holler* (New York: Vintage Books, 1994) 165.

[37]Cleaver, *Soul on Ice*, 64.

[38]McCall, *Makes Me Wanna Holler*, 165.

that I've left the streets. Yet when I consider white America and the way it's treated blacks, our random rage in the old days makes perfect sense to me. Looking back, it's easy to understand how it all got started."[39] For McCall, the beginning lies ominously in the working class neighborhood he grew up in Portsmouth, Virginia. Most of the individuals who lived there were blue-collar workers or active or retired military personnel; many had not completed high school or attended college. A good student and a well-adjusted child, McCall succumbs quickly to the subtle and overt forms of racism that mark his early elementary educational experience in a predominantly white school. This consciousness spawns a formidable rage that McCall transfers with him to the all-black middle school he enrolls in when his family relocates to Cavalier Manor. McCall speaks of the antagonistic relationship that many of its residents had with the poor whites who lived nearby in Academy Park. Night raids were common during McCall's tenure in Cavalier Manor, and the ditch that separated this neighborhood from the main thoroughfare to the city reinforced the separatist tendencies of a city intent on keeping its blacks in place.

McCall admits that his fascination with the drug culture and the gangsta life propelled him into criminal activity. These "bonding" activities, weak attempts at establishing a personage—a manhood rudimentarily established in the excess of violence—circumscribes the limits of McCall's psychic vision. By the time he was out of high school, he had engaged in gang violence, drug dealing, drug use, and armed robbery. His eventual incarceration comes as a result of his slow spiraling into no man's land, that space where many young black men feel like they are "bouncing around like pinballs in a machine, wondering if the world was fucked up or if [they are]; wondering why [they] were

---

[39]Ibid., 4.

being pushed into the backseat of life and couldn't get at the wheel."[40] This pinball machine, an extension of the underbelly of gender politics that traps young black men in the racialized conundrum of masculine sensibilities, precipitates McCall's subjugation. In this cultural prism, McCall is caught between refracted images of himself as it relates to the isms of white America, and a self-image grounded in his own cultural experience of illusory power. As McCall would later presume, such images fuel caustic behavior that leads nowhere: "If you're the only person riding in a car, and you're not driving, there's nothing to do but crash."[41] And crash he did.

In April 1975, McCall was convicted of the armed robbery of a white-owned convenience store and sentenced to twelve years in prison. It is here that McCall's racial consciousness reconstitutes itself as he becomes acutely aware of the predicament facing many young black men. The epigraph heading his chapter "Denial" charts the genesis of his journey through the prison system, and allows McCall to fuse the political with the personal as he reveals the undercurrent of institutionalized racism that reinforces the prison-parole-prison cycle:

> Blackmen born in the U.S. and fortunate enough to live past the age of eighteen are conditioned to accept the inevitability of prison. For most of us, it simply is the next phase in a sequence of humiliations. Being born a slave in a captive society and never experiencing any objective basis for expectation had the effect of preparing me for the progressively traumatic misfortunes that lead

---

[40]Ibid., 123.
[41]Ibid.

so many blackmen to the prison gate. I was prepared for
prison. It required only minor psychic adjustments.[42]

McCall's choice of epigraphs is telling and Jackson's words
are haunting. These writers illuminate what Malcolm, Cleaver,
and others have reiterated before: that the rite-of-passage for
young black men leads through prison, and thus prison—and all of
its isms—are part of the maturation process for young black male
adulthood.[43]

In connecting the prison experience to the history of slavery, Jackson, and subsequently McCall, makes the easy transition
from physical enslavement to mental enslavement. McCall's
references to the number of black men in his prison holding cell
(they are all black), and his observations that most, if not all, of
the prison guards are white, demonstrate how the prison system
replicates the social hierarchy of the previous chattel bondage
system of yesteryear. Moreover, the strains placed on one's
manhood (some black men are sexually "turned out" and
prostituted behind the wall) leads this critic to believe that not
only is the intent of the prison system to break down or
"reform" the condemned man, driving him mad in his own
body—this system is also intent on restructuring the very essence
of that person so that difference becomes exploited in a manner
that supports the sexual fantasies of those in charge. In one
instance, McCall recalls the activities of a white prison guard who
quietly preyed on one homosexual inmate: "He [the guard]
escorted the inmate to the back of the building, toward the
solitary-confinement cells. They remained there a good half hour

---

[42]From George Jackson, *Soledad Brother* (Chicago: Lawrence Hill Books,
1994) as quoted in McCall, *Makes Me Wanna Holler*, 149.
[43]Recent statistics from the US Justice Department reveal that there are
more black men in prison than in college, and a large number of the prison
population are high school dropouts. Of these, many are unable to read.

before the guard returned the inmate to his cell. It didn't take a rocket scientist to figure out what they had done."[44] In another instance, McCall describes the fears associated with gang rape and the parceling out of men who engaged in sexual activities to gain respect on the yard or get protection from one particular faction or gang in prison: "It fed a macho notion widely accepted in the joint: That a guy was even *more* of a man if he could 'flip' another man, turn him into a homosexual. They also called it 'breaking him down.' If they thought they spotted a mental weakness that they could exploit, they'd chip and chisel at it until they got results. Sometimes it took months before they got a breakthrough; sometimes it took years, which was no big deal for somebody doing time."[45] Reminiscent of the slave breaker, these men engage in spirit breaking and a subtle form of internalized racism as the conditions under which they are incarcerated cause them to turn on each other in an attempt to gain access to power and prestige. McCall's attention to the sexual activities that occur behind prison walls may seem displaced at first, but if one looks closer, it clearly reveals the close association between myth making and reality. Just as the slavemaster Mr. Garner in Toni Morrison's *Beloved* engaged in "man-making" on the Sweet Home plantation—he declared that his "niggers is men every one of em...bought em thataway, raised em thataway"[46]—yet he denied them the very natural process of the company of female companionship—the penal code system "raises" men to be brutal shadows of themselves, devoid of the capacity to love or engage in heterosexual activity with a woman should they choose to do so. The sinister reality of this predicament is that the genealogical bloodline of African Americans ceases to exist. "If you kill the male, you kill the species," declares Matthew McConahay's

---

[44]McCall, *Makes Me Wanna Holler*, 172.
[45]Ibid., 195.
[46]Toni Morrison, *Beloved* (New York: Penguin Books, 1987) 10.

character in the movie *Reign of Fire*. And indeed, the descxualization of thc black man in prison ensures the haunting predicament of this statement.[47]

McCall and Cleaver's quests for sanity in a country that does not acknowledge their personhood represents the journey of many black men who seek to find themselves in a world intent on colonizing their bodies, their material possessions, their very soul. The Higher Uneducation Cleaver speaks of in *Soul on Ice* is indicative of not only prison life itself but also the education found in the spoken and unspoken experiences of black men in the United States: the quiet surveillance of their activities in grocery stores, in malls, in suburban neighborhoods; the unacknowledged acceptance of their humanity and personhood in elevators, in "random" traffic stops, in the hallowed halls of academia. If the condemned body is, as Michel Foucault reminds us, the instrument of power that allows the prison system to enslave the essence of the soul,[48] then reclaiming this (criminalized) body through the channels of the mind is key to assessing the legacy of struggle in this country for men who are imprisoned. But more important, in analyzing the ways in which these texts call and respond to each other, we can better assess the black man's odyssey in this country, and more acutely determine his complicated and troubled desire to *be*.

---

[47]Editor Tara T. Green also makes this connection with Etheridge Knight's poem "The Idea of Ancestry," as she and Knight both conclude that the *denial* of ancestry reaffirms this predicament.

[48]Michel Foucault, *Discipline and Punish: The Birth of the Person* (New York: Vintage Books, 1977) 29.

Works Cited

Auther, Jennifer et al. "'He Was a Symbol': Eldridge Cleaver
    Dies at 62." *CNN News*.
    www.cnn.com/US/9805/01/cleaver.late.obit, 1 May 1998.
Butler, Robert. *Contemporary African American Fiction: The Open
    Journey*. Madison: Fairleigh Dickinson University Press,
    1998.
Cleaver, Eldridge. *Soul on Ice*, New York: Dell Publishing, 1991.
Didion, Joan. *The White Album*. New York: Simon and Schuster,
    1979.
Douglass, Frederick. *Narrative of the Life of Frederick Douglass, an
    American Slave*. 1845. Reprint, New York: W. W. Norton
    and Company, 1997.
Foucault, Michel. *Discipline & Punish: The Birth of the Prison*. New
    York: Vintage Books, 1977.
Henry, Joseph. "The Public, Spiritual, and Humanistic Odyssey
    of Malcolm X: A Critical Bibliographical Debate." *Iowa
    Journal of Literary Studies* 4/1 (1983): 77–93.
Jackson, George. *Soledad Brother*. 1970. Reprint, Chicago:
    Lawrence Hill Books, 1994.
Jardine, Gail. "To Be Black, Male, and Conscious: Race, Rage,
    and Manhood in America." *American Quarterly* 48/2 (June
    1996): 385–93.
Knight, Etheridge. "The Idea of Ancestry." In *The Norton
    Anthology of African American Literature*, edited by Henry
    Louis Gates, Jr., and Nellie Y. McKay, 1867–68. New York:
    W. W. Norton & Company, Inc., 1997.
Lyne, William. "No Accident: From Black Power to Black Box
    Office." *African American Review* 34/1 (Spring 2000): 39–59.
McCall, Nathan. *Makes Me Wanna Holler*. New York: Vintage
    Books, 1994.

Morrison, Toni. *Beloved*. New York: Penguin Books, 1987.

Reed, Ishmael. Preface. In *Soul on Ice*. New York: Dell Publishing, 1991.

Sanchez-Eppler, Karen. *Touching Liberty: Abolition, Feminism, and the Politics of the Body*. Berkeley: University of California Press, 1993.

Smith, Sidonie. *Where I'm Bound: Patterns of Slavery and Freedom in Black American Autobiography*. Westport CT: Greenwood Press, 1974.

Wright, Richard. "How 'Bigger' Was Born." In *Native Son*, 431–62. New York: HarperPerennial, 1998.

Lessons before Dying:
The Contemporary Confined
Character-in-Process

Dana A. Williams

In the opening essay of *The Furious Voice for Freedom: Essays on Life*, Leon Forrest writes, "I believe that in Afro-American literature, *reinvention* has been the basic hallmark of the transformation of those black novelists coming after Richard Wright."[1] He defines *re-creation* or *reinvention* as "the powerful use of the imagination to take a given form and make something that appears completely new of it—that creates within the reading...audience a sense of the magical meaning of life transformed."[2] Forrest's concept of reinvention comes, of course, in conversation with Henry L. Gates, Jr.'s idea of signifyin(g). As Gates notes, signifyin(g), like reinvention, "entails formal revision and an intertextual relation."[3] Because of the "formal manner in which texts seem concerned to address their antecedents," signifyin(g), which involves "repetition, with a signal difference," is indeed a viable theory through which to

---

[1]Leon Forrest, *The Furious Voice for Freedom: Essays on Life* (Wakefield RI: Asphodel, 1994) 28.

[2]Ibid., 10.

[3]Henry L. Gates, Jr., *The Signifyin(g) Monkey: A Theory of African-American Literary Criticism* (New York: Oxford University Press, 1988) 51.

read African-American literary texts, particularly those, as Forrest suggests, following Richard Wright. If, as Gates contends, the recurrence of revisions of tropes is central to African-American literature—and, hence, its adoption of signifyin(g) as one of its fundamental features—then one of the earliest tropes that would logically be repeatedly revised is the trope of confinement. Narratives from Olaudah Equiano to Frederick Douglass to Harriet Jacobs all address the trope of confinement as it relates to their enslavement and subsequent freedom. Jacobs's *Incidents in the Life of a Slave Girl* is also among the first of those narratives involving confinement on multiple levels. Her literal seven-year confinement within a hole above her grandmother's living quarters, which she endures as a means of rejecting the confines of slavery, arguably emerges in more contemporary literature revised as confinement underground.[4]

As Gates suggests, "authors produce meaning in part by revising formal patterns of representation in their fictions. This production of meaning...simultaneously involves a positioning or a critiquing both of received literary conventions and of the subject matter represented in canonical texts of the tradition."[5] Few texts are more canonical in African-American literature than the emancipatory narratives, and few tropes recur with more frequency than the trope of confinement in contemporary African-American literature. From Wright's *Native Son* to Ralph Ellison's *Invisible Man* to Leon Forrest's *The Bloodworth Orphans* (which aggressively engages with Ellison's *Invisible Man*) to Ernest Gaines's *A Lesson before Dying* (which is in conversation with Wright's *Native Son*),[6] contemporary African-American

---

[4] I am thinking here of Wright's "The Man Who Lived Underground" and Ellison's *Invisible Man*, where characters are literally physically underground.

[5] Forrest, *Furious Voice*, 113.

[6] On a number of occasions, Gaines has suggested that he was not influenced by Wright or by *Native Son* in his writing of *Lesson*; see interviews reprinted in John Lowe's *Conversations with Ernest Gaines* (Jackson: University

male authors use the trope of confinement to suggest that "freedom comes from human beings, rather than from laws and institutions."[7] Arguably, their attempt to investigate this supposition in their literature adopts a pattern not that dissimilar from the development of the hero as a character-in-process.[8] With variation, these authors' characters-in-process all follow a specific pattern through which they ultimately transcend their confinement: first, their confinement either forces or encourages them to examine the "self"; second, following their self-examination, they (re)affirm their humanity or individuality, which, in most cases, has been denied them; third, now believers in their humanity or defenders of their individuality, they investigate strategies of survival whereby they might be able to have others acknowledge their humanity or individuality as well; fourth and finally, they either attempt to assert their (re)defined "self" in the context of the community, or they accept their fates (often death) but now as redefined men.

A close reading of "Fate," the final section of *Native Son*, reveals Bigger Thomas as the prototype for the contemporary confined character-in-process. Having been captured and beaten

---

Press of Mississippi, 1995). Rather, Gaines argues that his idea for writing the novel was most heavily influenced by the story of a young man on death row in Louisiana; see Gaines's collected essays in *Mozart and Leadbelly*, eds. Marcia Gaudet, Reggie Young, and Ernest Gaines (New York: Knopf, 2005). Two critical texts, in particular, however argue (perhaps too aggressively) that Wright's influence on Gaines is evident throughout *Lesson*; see Keith Clark, *Black Manhood in James Baldwin, Ernest J. Gaines, and August Wilson* (Urbana: University of Illinois Press, 2002) and Madelyn Jablon, *Black Metafiction: Self-Consciousness in African American Literature* (Iowa City: University of Iowa Press, 1997).

[7]Forrest, *Furious Voice*, 65.

[8]I made this recognition after reading Forrest's "Luminosity from the Lower Frequencies" in *Furious Voice*, where he notes the influence of Kenneth Burke and Lord Raglan on Ellison's character-in-process progression. He notes especially the influence of Raglan's *The Hero* and Burke's notion that a pattern could be employed to achieve character-in-process progression through the formula of purpose, passion, and perception.

by the police for the alleged rape and murder of Mary Dalton and Bessie Mears, Bigger sits aimlessly in a cell at the Eleventh Street Police Station. In spite of the police's greatest attempts, Bigger refuses to speak or to eat. When he finally begins to "come out into the world again,"[9] he is still so disconnected from everything that he claims that they could take him to the electric chair at that moment for all he cared. He does eventually come to, and his first fully articulated words, ironically, involve communication. As one who is portrayed as and believed (by his captors) to be more animal-like than human, Bigger shifts from silence and grunting to a verbal request for a newspaper so that he can read about himself.

Isolated from the mainstream world for most of his life and, now, isolated in his cell of confinement, Bigger longs to see himself in the context of larger society. What he quickly realizes, however, is that while he has indeed become a real part of society, it is not in the context he desired. Nor does society represent him truthfully. Instead, he is portrayed as a beastly member of "a poor darky family of a shiftless and immoral variety" who avoids earlier confinement in a chain gang only because of his youth.[10] Angered by the comments about himself, Bigger debates returning to a conscious state of unconsciousness. But before he resolves to shut the world out once again, he is visited by Reverend Hammond, the pastor of his mother's church. And as Reverend Hammond prays for him and, again, places him in the context of a broader society—in this case, a society of religious believers—Bigger feels "a sense of guilt deeper than that which even his murder of Mary had made him feel."[11] Seeing Reverend Hammond's eyes and knowing that the reverend believes that he had a soul that could be saved causes

---

[9]Richard Wright, *Native Son* (New York: HarperPerennial, 1993) 321.
[10]Ibid., 323.
[11]Ibid., 328.

Bigger to suspect possibilities of humanity for himself. Never having experienced this feeling in any meaningful way before, Bigger wonders: "Why should this thing rise now to plague him after he had pressed a pillow of fear and hate over its face to smother it to death? To those who wanted to kill him he was not human, not included in that picture of Creation; and that was why he had killed it. To live, he had created a new world for himself, and for that he was to die."[12] This brief passage reveals that Bigger's life struggle is largely with both his own and other people's acknowledgment and denial of his humanity. Innately, he had believed in it, only to realize that the world that mattered denied it. So when he sees its possibilities again through Reverend Hammond, he resolves, once again, to kill it. He imagines he can do this rather easily until he encounters Jan and Max, both of whom also claim to believe in his worth.

In spite of the fact that Bigger implicates Jan as being guilty of killing his girlfriend Mary, Jan tells Bigger that he is not angry with him and that he wants to help him. While he is confined, Jan claims to realize that it is Bigger's right to hate him and that his white face probably made Bigger feel guilty; so, on some levels, it is Jan who is the guilty one. Wondering whether Jan's offer to help him is a trap, Bigger begins to examine his self and his worth again: "He looked at Jan and saw a white face, but an honest face. This white man believed in him, and the moment he felt that belief he felt guilty again; but in a different sense now....For the first time in his life a white man became a human being to him; and the reality of Jan's humanity came in a stab of remorse: he had killed what this man loved and had hurt him."[13] Bigger's acknowledgment of Jan's humanity foreshadows his acknowledgment of his own. While the significance of Jan's whiteness to Bigger's acceptance of the possibilities within

---

[12]Ibid., 328.
[13]Ibid., 333.

himself may be problematic, it is clear that he begins to examine himself meaningfully because others, both Jan and Reverend Hammond, believe in him.

Still doubtful of the usefulness of any attempt to move beyond his self-imposed isolation, Bigger and Jan have the following exchange:

> "Forget me," [Bigger] mumbled.
> "I can't," Jan said.
> "It's over for me," Bigger said.
> "Don't you believe in yourself?"
> "Naw," Bigger whispered tensely.
> "You believed enough to kill. You thought you were settling something, or you wouldn't've killed," Jan said.
> Bigger stared and did not answer. Did this man believe in him *that* much?[14]

Max, who has been waiting outside, then enters, and Bigger, still doubtful of Jan's intentions, repeatedly tells Max that he has no money. Eventually, he accepts Max's help, and it is during and after conversations he has with Max that he engages in the most beneficial self-examination and reaffirmation of his humanity. Significantly, however, thoughts of his family and his desire to accept Reverend Hammond's belief in him prepare him for full acceptance of his worth. After seeing his mother, brother, and sister, Bigger realizes that neither his life nor his actions exist in isolation after all: "He had lived and acted on the assumption that he was alone, and now he saw that he had not been. What he had done made others suffer. No matter how much he would long for them to forget him, they would not be able to. His family was a part of him, not only in blood, but in spirit."[15] He struggles with

---

14Ibid., 334.
15Ibid., 345.

this realization, along with the hope of the cross Reverend
Hammond gives him, until he sees a cross burning on the roof.

Knowing that the cross has something to do with him, he
immediately thinks of the cross he now possesses, the cross of
Jesus, "for him, a cross for everyone...showing how to die, how to
love and live the eternal life."[16] Though he never admits or
accepts it, he explores religion as a possible strategy of survival in
a world that could deny a man of his humanity.[17] But then he
hears the crowd yelling "Burn 'im," "Kill 'im!" and he feels
betrayed that the cross of Christ and the cross of the Ku Klux
Klan could be one in the same. He snatches the chain from his
neck and remarks, first, that he can die without a cross and,
second, that he has no soul.

> Never again did he want to feel anything like hope.
> That was what was wrong; he had let that preacher talk to
> him until somewhere in him he had begun to feel that
> maybe something could happen. Well, something *had*
> happened: the cross the preacher had hung around his
> throat had been turned in front of his eyes....A small hard
> core in him resolved never again to trust anybody or
> anything. Not even Jan or Max...whatever he thought or
> did from now on would have to come from him alone, or
> not at all.[18]

And this is, indeed, how Bigger comes to accept his fate—on his
own terms.

---

[16]Ibid., 390.

[17]While Bigger has clearly abandoned religion as a real possibility for
survival long before he commits his murders, his disappointment in the public's
use of the cross as a symbol of hate so soon after he reluctantly accepts the cross
from Rev. Hammond suggests to me that, at the very least, he briefly
reconsidered religion as a possible source of comfort and survival.

[18]Wright, *Native Son*, 394.

After talking to Max about the things he had hoped for himself but that had been denied because of his race and class, he has a sense of peace he has not known before. He realizes that "he had spoken to Max as he had never spoken to anyone in his life; not even to himself,"[19] and he begins to get angry and to believe that Max has tricked him. But he quickly realizes that "Max had not compelled him to talk; he had talked of his own accord, prodded by...a curiosity about his own feelings."[20] Although Max's questioning is indeed the catalyst for Bigger's self-revelation, he achieves it largely by himself. Notably, this is frequently a point of contention for critics of the novel. But as James A. Miller notes in "Bigger Thomas's Quest for Voice and Audience in Richard Wright's *Native Son*," Bigger is articulate even before he encounters Max. And while Bigger's voice "falters in the presence of white people,"[21] ultimately it is Bigger, not Max, who is concerned with Bigger's personal fate and who finally articulates the truth of Bigger's life since, even at the novel's end, "there is a question of whether Max finally understands Bigger Thomas."[22]

Ultimately, Bigger blends the final two stages of the contemporary confined character-in-process almost seamlessly. In his assertion of his redefined "self," he accepts his fate while he simultaneously realizes the possibilities for survival. "He wondered if it were possible that after all everybody in the world felt alike? ...For the first time in his life he had gained a pinnacle of feeling upon which he could stand and see vague relations that he had never dreamed of. If that white looming mountain of hate were not a mountain at all, but people, people like himself...then

---

[19]Ibid., 417.

[20]Ibid., 417.

[21]James A. Miller, "Bigger Thomas's Quest for Voice and Audience in Richard Wright's *Native Son*," *Callaloo* 28/3 (Summer 1986): 504.

[22]Ibid., 505.

he was faced with a high hope the like of which he had never thought could be."[23] Having outright rejected religion as a viable strategy of survival for himself, he instead embraces the one truth that his oppressors were most unwilling to admit—that people are more alike than they are different. Once he realizes and accepts this, he has no need for Max's lengthy speech, though, at times, it echoes Bigger's revelation. He accepts the fact that he was unconscious of his belief in his own humanity for far too long. Ultimately, he realizes that deep down that belief was always there—so much so that it prompted him to kill. Thus, he willingly confesses to Max that "What I killed for, I am!"[24]—and he is, subsequently, able to walk to his death like a man.

While Bigger's prison confinement, like the physical confinement of slavery, is involuntary, Ellison revises the trope of confinement and has his protagonist in *Invisible Man* choose to imprison himself. Initially, the Invisible Man is indeed hiding from pursuers, but eventually he openly chooses to stay underground and to write his story. Even so, he loosely follows the pattern of the confined character-in-process and uses his confinement to examine the "self," to affirm his individuality, to formulate survival strategies to ensure his success upon reemergence, and to prepare to reassert his re-defined self in the context of the community. Logically, it is a sub-plot of confinement, the infamous Golden Day scene that occurs in chapter 3, that foreshadows all that the Invisible Man will experience, particularly as these experiences relate to his quest for identity and to others' denial of it.

As one of the naïve acts that initiates the Invisible Man's dismissal from the college and thus thwarts his plan to become the next Booker T. Washington, the narrator's choice to take

---

[23]Wright, *Native Son*, 418.
[24]Ibid., 501.

Mr. Norton, the trustee left to his care, inside the Golden Day while the patients from the mental hospital are making their weekly visit to the bar is one that he comes to regret but one that he must also acknowledge as informative. While inside the bar, Norton and the narrator encounter a group of veterans who have been institutionalized because they dared to exceed the narrow limits of success society has for them. After he rather effortlessly diagnoses Norton's rare condition—one that only the finest specialist in the country has previously been able to diagnose—one of the vets who is a former doctor informs Norton that he too was a specialist, though now he is "an inmate of a semimadhouse."[25] Like his fellow vets who are also confined to a quasimental institution for their unwillingness to comply with Jim Crow laws after they return to the United States from France, the doctor serves as a source of confusion for the narrator. While he thinks it is their weekly presence at the Golden Day that makes him feel uncomfortable, it is really the vets' confinement as prisoners, not as patients, that disturbs the narrator: "They were supposed to be members of the professions toward which at various times [he] vaguely aspired [him]self....Sometimes it appeared as though they played some vast and complicated game with [him] and the rest of the school folk, a game whose goal was laughter and whose rules and subtleties [he] could never grasp."[26] The rules and subtleties he can never grasp are arguably those of confinement—confinement of black middle-class identity and mobility to that which white America deems appropriate.

Ellison's imagery is rich throughout the chapter—the irony of the bar's name the *Golden Day*,[27] the set-back clocks,

---

[25]Ralph Ellison, *Invisible Man* (New York: Vintage, 1972) 88.

[26]Ibid., 73.

[27]Ellison's use of The Golden Day as the name of his bar mocks the concept of a "golden day" for America as espoused by Ralph Waldo Emerson, Henry David Thoreau, and Henry James and by Lewis Mumford's *The Golden*

Supercargo's pun on super ego and the overwhelming whiteness that accompanies his supervisory presence—but it is the vet's commentary to Norton and the narrator that proves most meaningful. After telling them that he was driven out of town by ten men in masks at midnight for saving a human life, the doctor tells the narrator that knowledge could bring him neither wealth nor dignity. When the Invisible Man fails to understand the vet's allegory of the limitations he will face as a black man, the vet looks to Norton and remarks of the narrator: "he has eyes and ears and a good distended African nose, but he fails to understand the simple facts of life....Nothing has meaning. He takes it in but he doesn't digest it....Already he's learned to repress not only his emotions but his humanity. He's invisible, a walking personification of the Negative, the most perfect achievement of your dreams, sir! The mechanical man!"[28] The doctor is, of course, referring to Norton's (or white America's) misplaced control of the students' fate and to the narrator's failure to see this control. Instead, he accepts it and is thus rendered so mechanical that he is ultimately invisible as an individual.

Because he tells his story in retrospect, the narrator examines the "self" throughout the novel. But as in *Native Son*, where Bigger's compliance with the confined character-in-process pattern becomes most obvious near the end of the text, Ellison's confined protagonist uses the last few pages of the novel, especially the epilogue, to reveal his critical findings. The novel almost comes full circle, with the narrator still questioning the meaning of his dying grandfather's words about being a traitor and his command to the narrator to live with his "head in the lion's mouth."[29] Though he can never be sure what his

---

Day: A Study of American Experience and Culture (New York: Boni and Liveright, 1926).

[28]Ellison, *Invisible Man*, 92.

[29]Ibid., 16.

grandfather meant exactly, the narrator does come to reaffirm his humanity and to assert his individuality by contemplating both his own life and his grandfather's life. He confesses: "Once I thought my grandfather incapable of thoughts about humanity, but I was wrong. Why should an old slave use such a phrase as "this and this or this has made me more human," as I did in my arena speech? Hell, he never had any doubts about his humanity—that was left to his 'free' offspring."[30] This realization prompts the Invisible Man to end his hibernation and to return to the world with the resolve that perhaps "even an invisible man has a socially responsible role to play."[31]

But he can only return to the world with sufficient confidence because he has investigated a number of potential survival strategies. Ultimately, again, it is thoughts of his grandfather's words that free him, though he first tries the old reliables, including flight, music, liquor, and education: "I hibernated. I got away from it all. But that wasn't enough. I couldn't be still even in hibernation. Because, damn it, there's the mind, the *mind*. It wouldn't let me rest. Gin, jazz and dreams were not enough. Books were not enough. My belated appreciation of the crude joke that kept me running was not enough. And my mind revolved again and again back to my grandfather."[32] When he realizes that the "cream of the joke" (his grandfather's admonition) is that people are all connected, even as all men are different and divided, he asserts that the fate of humanity is "to become one, and yet many."[33] Thus, he accepts his fate as one who might be, at times, rendered invisible and also as one who must, nevertheless, return to the world and be socially responsible.

---

[30]Ibid., 567.
[31]Ibid., 568.
[32]Ibid., 560.
[33]Ibid., 564.

Leon Forrest has his protagonist, Nathaniel Witherspoon, be similarly influenced by an ancestral presence in *The Bloodworth Orphans* as the novel's ancestral figure, Noah Grandberry, articulates a *truth* similar to that which the Invisible Man has come to accept as the essence of what his grandfather tries to express to him metaphorically. While Forrest's first novel, *There Is a Tree More Ancient than Eden*, and his second, *The Bloodworth Orphans*, are both in dialogue with the magnum opus of his literary mentor (Ellison), the final chapters of *The Bloodworth Orphans* overtly expand and revise *Invisible Man*'s Golden Day chapter and its epilogue. Like the Invisible Man, Noah and Nathaniel have some level of choice regarding their confinement. Both are being held captive in the Refuge Hospital for their alleged connections to Forest County's trickster W. W. W. Ford, but Nathaniel and Noah frequently escape and return to the isolation ward where the men are being held for experimental purposes. Nathaniel, for instance, robs two meat stores with a toy gun; he steals medicine from the ICU ward for Noah's cold; the two men lift each other up to the roof of the hospital to watch the stars at night; and they create a contraption that allows them to steal cartons of milk from nearby window sills. Yet they never try to escape, arguably because Noah must first explain his life to Nathaniel and then because they must investigate strategies of survival before they complete their reentry into the world.

Like the veterans who are institutionalized by a Jim Crow system in *Invisible Man*, the residents of Forest County's Refuge Hospital are former middle-class artists and professionals who have gone mad after being exploited for their talent and then denied dignity. One such character is the jazz great Ironwood Ramble. Ironically, before Nathaniel is captured, he would often sneak into the hospital just to hear Ironwood play. His music takes all of the residents to places otherwise unknown, and, as a survival strategy, it orders their chaos and leads them to some semblance of wholeness. The tragedy of Ironwood's genius, however, is that he is exploited and controlled for so long on the outside—which Forrest expresses metaphorically by having Ironwood's horns turn into a visage of corroded chains that are carted off in huge money-sacks—that he may be better off literally confined than metaphorically free. Even as "three gigantic goons" come shrieking at him and place chains around his ankles, three "older trustees" inform Nathaniel that Ironwood is taken away every night to a quarantined section of rooms where at least he is peaceful and free, "not like out in the world where he is enslaved" and people slip "heroin to him to make money off of his body."[34] Even Ironwood, the men claim, when "he is in his best frame of mind, knows that he is better off" in the Refuge Hospital than "out in hell."[35] Hearing this, Noah and Nathaniel contemplate the usefulness of their plan to escape after three months of confinement and just two days before they are to be subjected to a battery of tests.

In order for them to have a reasonable chance of surviving, they must successfully navigate their journeys as confined characters-in-process. Noah's self-examination takes on the form of storytelling, while Nathaniel's occurs as he is compelled to see his and his family's likeness to Noah and his experiences. Noah's story also offers much needed insight into Forrest's recurring trickster figure Ford. Left orphaned by his mother, who hangs herself after killing his father for repeatedly mistreating and exploiting her sexually, Noah informs Nathaniel that Ford, Noah's great-grandfather, the fortuneteller who uses the young Noah to exploit clients, and the Seer who claims to allow Noah to speak to his dead mother are all one and the same. As Nathaniel bemoans Noah's tendencies toward tall-tales, one of

---

[34]Leon Forrest, *The Bloodworth Orphans* (New York: Random House, 1977) 316.

[35]Ibid.

the lessons Nathaniel learns is that the real and the imagined are sometimes interchangeable. But the larger lesson, one that adopts the Invisible Man's language and ideology, comes in the form of satire and takes ideas about whiteness and light as its theme. Nathaniel must outright reject this satirical commentary, even as the institution's administrator presents it as scientific truth, and formulate his own ideas about "the light" instead.

Transformed almost completely from the form in which confinement appears in *Invisible Man*, Forrest's confinement scenes are nearly carnivalesque. As Nathaniel and Noah are in the middle of their talks about Ford, they are interrupted by a "power explosion of sound."[36] A Vietnamese midget, dubbed Hoo-Chardo, appears with a police dog almost as tall as he and begins to talk to them about the definition of *light* and *whiteness*. When Nathaniel comments that he thought *whiteness* was the absence of color and not that which light serves, which is what Chardo claims, Chardo tells Nathaniel, "Well, see, that's why you are here, in order to free your mind of this misinformation. Light and truth are rather slow trickling down into the interior, or rather, shall we say the hard-core, which is part of our thesis."[37] He then goes on, claiming to demonstrate his thesis to them: "You see this prism; now, notice how the prism separates and divides and subdivides the light into all its different basic colors. But purely separates, fairly, clearly. Each color of course has its own autonomy, almost personality, inherent, you might say; although we do discourage...misdirected individualism. Each color is imbued with a different wavelength and frequency."[38] Then he tells them that if he is giving them too much information too fast, the one thing they must remember above all else is "that White Light is a cluster of all those different frequencies which

---

[36]Ibid., 288.
[37]Ibid., 291.
[38]Ibid., 291.

the prism sorts out."[39] Strip everything down to its original form, he claims, and what you will return to is whiteness "at the dawn of creation."[40]

Chardo's comments stand in complete opposition to the Invisible Man's craving for individualism and his revelation about how man is at base essentially and inescapably connected. But "only in division is there true health," the Invisible Man comes to believe; "diversity is the word. Let man keep his many parts and you'll have no tyrant states."[41] As he complains about man's passion toward conformity, he notes that unless he rebels, he will end up becoming white, "which is not a color but the lack of one."[42] If they are to avoid such a fate, Noah and Nathaniel, for whom the Invisible Man seems also to speak for on a *lower frequency*, must choose wisely as they examine the catalogue of strategies the trickster Ford uses to reinvent himself repeatedly and to avoid the traps of conformity.

One such strategy is the power of transformation. According to Noah, Ford is a serial hermaphrodite who, like the mythical Tiresias, changes back and forth from male to female every seven years as a result of seeing snakes copulate. He also transforms himself from salesman to fortuneteller to preacher to seer whenever doing so is necessary or convenient. Noah and Nathaniel adopt this imperative to transform to sustain and to entertain themselves in the Refuge Hospital. When they find a closet full of children's toys, they remake them into adult games of chance. They transform straightjackets, sheets, blankets, and pillowslips into a ladder, which Nathaniel uses to scale the sixty-story building. They dip Nathaniel's hospital tunic in paint and use coloring sets they find in the closet to transform the tunic

---

[39]Ibid., 292.
[40]Ibid., 292.
[41]Ellison, *Invisible Man*, 563.
[42]Ibid., 564.

into a bright dashiki to disguise his confined status when he escapes to get food. The more their supplies run out, the more inventive they are forced to become. So what Nathaniel, as Noah's "young rookie" apprentice, must learn from this experience is that no matter how dire the situation may seem, he must never allow himself to be so overwhelmed with his condition that he becomes consumed by it and thus rendered immobile.

To teach Nathaniel this lesson, Noah tells Nathaniel the story of how Noah successfully escaped a band of Ford's followers, only to awaken on a Mississippi border to two highway cops with their guns pointed at his eyes and bloodhounds on their sides: "that was when I discovered that the problem is not the energy crisis, nor a bankrupt blood bank, nor bloodletting, nor hardening of the arteries, in the life-prolonging nervous system, but, Spoons, how to keep that old blood circulating, no matter what blood group or bloodlines your streams shoot through...that's the best way I know to avoid a bloodbath, and a low blood count."[43] What Noah tells Nathaniel, in essence, is that when it comes down to it, all that matters is knowing how to stay alive. One can indeed become overwhelmed with trying to locate or to define the origins of the social, economic, and political crises; with anger and rage, hence the blood bank and the hardened arteries; or with despair about suffering, hence the low blood count. One way to avoid such failures is to move forward constantly so as not to lose the driving force of life. Constant action offers one of the few chances of survival.

And this is what Noah boldly announces near the end of the novel when the two men prepare to reenter the chaotic world of Forest County. As Nathaniel bemoans not being able to free Ironwood and complains of the loss of his friends, who turn out to

---

[43]Forrest, *The Bloodworth Orphans*, 338–39.

be Noah's siblings, Noah screams at Nathaniel, who is clearly too caught up in his own emotions to move forward: "You've got to stop sobbing over the past. Indeed, the only way I've found to stop the hounding voices...is through Action. *And* we've got to move forward now. You were prepared to move out a few minutes ago, yet the mention of the personally deceased ones always throws you into deep depression."[44] Even as Noah chastises Nathaniel, he forces him to contemplate the past but to move beyond it quickly rather than dwelling on it. He immediately gives him a parachute, which he has stolen from the helicopter service section, and they descend "into a cathedral of ritual warfare."[45] And even though there are gang wars all around them, and the body of the mayor is burning, they, like the Invisible Man, know that they must try to "give pattern to the chaos which lives within the pattern of...certainty,"[46] if for no other reason than to save the sobbing babe they find in a boot box as they flee the city in a stolen police car.

Because they have access to and awareness and acceptance of more cultural strategies of survival than any of the other confined protagonists—from musical impulses to storytelling to the power of transformation—Noah and Nathaniel are perhaps better equipped to accept their fate than Bigger Thomas or the Invisible Man. They also have each other, while Bigger and the Invisible Man are ultimately isolated. Community thus holds more significance and has a more formidable presence in *The Bloodworth Orphans* than in either of the other two novels. Again, Forrest seems to be riffing on an idea espoused by the Invisible Man, who realizes that any *we* is a part of any *them* "as well as apart from *them* and subject to die when *they* died."[47] Highlighting

[44]Ibid., 382.
[45]Ibid., 382.
[46]Ellison, *Invisible Man*, 567.
[47]Ibid., 562; emphasis added.

the interconnectedness of the seemingly distinct thus becomes a signal feature of Noah's lessons to Nathaniel, although connecting Noah's stories to his own family history seems to be more natural than learned for Nathaniel. Even as he listens to Noah and attempts to glean something useful from Noah's tall tales, Nathaniel constantly seeks to insert himself and to integrate his history into the stories. In a novel overly concerned with the vulnerability of orphanhood and the detriments of motherlessness, redefining oneself in the context of and in relation to the community becomes essential.

Community is similarly important in Ernest Gaines's *A Lesson before Dying*. Consciously or unconsciously, Gaines's novel adopts *Native Son*'s inquiries into black humanity but allows affirmation to come through the black community. While the black community in *Native Son*—represented by Reverend Hammond and Bigger's family and friends—has a limited effect on Bigger's belief in his own humanity, in *A Lesson before Dying* the community—Grant, Jefferson's family, and the school children—ultimately offers Jefferson the courage he needs to walk to his death like a man. Bigger, of course, uses this same language about manhood and being able "to walk" to his execution, and both men are able to do so because, at the time of their deaths, they believe wholeheartedly in their humanity.

Even as the novels exhibit obvious parallels, Jefferson is drawn somewhat differently from Bigger. Jefferson, for one, is not guilty of the crimes for which he is being accused. Yet, this factor is of little significance since both authors suggest that innocence and guilt are inappropriate measures of humanity and inhumanity. Both men make bad choices under tremendous amounts of pressure, but neither should be judged as less human for his inability to reason quickly and effectively. Yet this is precisely why Jefferson's attorney argues that Jefferson should not be killed—not because he is innocence but because killing him would offer only as much justice as one could achieve killing a hog. So, while Max argues for Bigger's life on the basis of his inaccessibility to full humanity and the denial of his manhood by a capitalist society, Jefferson's attorney claims that Jefferson's life should be spared because he is more animal than human.[48]

> Gentlemen of the jury, look at this—this—this boy. I almost said man, but I can't say man. Oh, sure, he has reached the age of twenty-one, when we, civilized men, consider the male species has reached manhood, but who would call this—this—this a man? Not I... Look at the shape of [Jefferson's] skull, this face as flat as the palm of my hand.... A cornered animal to strike quickly out of fear, a trait inherited from his ancestors in the deepest jungle of blackest Africa—yes, yes, that he can do—but to plan...this skull here holds no plan.[49]

The defense does, at points, note that the jury should believe Jefferson's version of the episode for which he will be killed—that he had no idea Bear and Brother would try to rob the store (unlike Bigger and his friends, who do attempt to plan their robbery), that he did not kill the store owner, and that he took the liquor and the money because he panicked (as Bigger does when Mrs. Dalton enters Mary's room). But even as he proclaims Jefferson's innocence, the attorney denies his humanity and likens Jefferson to a hog. And it is an attempt to rectify this wrong that sets the formal *diegesis* of the novel and Jefferson's role as a confined character-in-process in motion.

---

[48]Notably, the legal strategy Max chooses to use for Bigger's trial is also heavily critiqued. See Miller, "Bigger Thomas's Quest," 505. The attorneys in both novels, in essence, argue that both protagonists' lives should be spared because, as black men, they have been denied full access to humanity.

[49]Ernest Gaines, *A Lesson before Dying* (New York: Vintage, 1994) 7.

While Gaines does not go to any lengths to suggest
Jefferson's confidence in his humanity before he is called a hog,
it is clear that the characterization has a dramatic effect on
Jefferson's idea of his "self." When Grant visits Jefferson alone
for the first time, they have the following exchange:

> "You hungry?" [Grant] asked.
> "You brought some corn?" [Jefferson] said.
> "Corn?"
> "That's what hogs eat..."[50]

Grant notices that Jefferson has not washed his face or
combed his hair in some days, and he is not wearing any shoes.
Then, Jefferson begins to grunt like a hog, while Grant
comments that the food he has brought is good:

> "Your nannan can sure cook," [Grant] said.
> "That's for youmans," [Jefferson] said.
> "You're a human being, Jefferson..."
> "I'm a old hog," he said. "Youmans don't stay in no
>   stall like this. I'm a old hog they fattening up to
>   kill."[51]

Even if he believed in himself and his humanity before, he
does not now, so his self-examination is almost in reverse of the
more typical character-in-process pattern. Instead of reaffirming
his humanity, his self-examination in confinement denies it.
What Grant must do, in his combination role of teacher and
pupil, is to find ways to help Jefferson rediscover his humanity
and to accept his fate. And it is his fulfillment of this challenge
that proves to be his and the readers' lesson before dying.

---

[50]Ibid., 82.
[51]Ibid., 83.

While the text does not offer a foolproof method by which Grant is able to get Jefferson to believe in himself again, it does suggest the importance of man's commitment to and connectedness with his community in his assessment of "self." Thus, Jefferson's relationship with his godmother, and the possibility that people who are not related to him or people he does not know especially well nevertheless care about him, help restore his faith in himself. He stops acting like a hog and begins to eat with his visitors because Grant reminds him of his obligation to make his godmother's life easier; he apologizes for disrespecting Grant's girlfriend Vivian because he realizes that she cares about him; and his first full statement that has nothing to do with his being characterized a hog is one of thanks to the community children, who send him pecans to eat and who later come to visit him. It is through his direct and indirect interaction with the community, then, that Jefferson gains the desire to express himself, which he does most effectively through writing.

At least two significant elements are at work during the chapter titled "Jefferson's Diary." First, Gaines simultaneously accepts and mocks the Enlightenment philosophy that man's distinctive characteristic is his ability to reason. Jefferson's attorney, who might be appropriately recognized as representing well-meaning but poorly informed white America, believes wholeheartedly in this philosophy, which is why he argues that Jefferson, because he has no skills of reasoning, should not be acknowledged as a man. Gaines rejects this philosophy clearly. Yet, he has Jefferson achieve manhood by reasoning himself into humanity. The entire diary thus becomes proof of his ability to reason, even if only minimally.

His entries move from almost purely observational to thoughtful. He is able to make this transition largely because of Grant. Jefferson writes, "mr wigin you say you like what i got here but you say you stil cant give me a a just a b cause you say i

aint gone dep in me yet an you kno i can if I try hard an when i ax
you what you mean deep in me you say jus say whats on my
mind...sometime mr wigin i just feel like tellin you i like you but
i dont know how to say this cause i aint never say it to nobody
before an nobody aint never say it to me."[52] But after visits from
the schoolchildren and other people in the community, Jefferson
is able to connect, through reasoning, why he is moved to tears
after their visits: "this was the firs time i cry when they lok that
door bahind me the very firs time an i jus set on my bunk cryin
but not let them see or yer me cause i didn want them think rong
but i was cryin cause of bok an the marble he giv me and cause o
the peple com to see me cause they hadn never done nothin like
that for me befor."[53] And he cries again when Grant tells him
that he will not be coming to see him any more, and, again,
Jefferson is able to connect his emotions to his actions: "im sory
i cry when you say you aint coming back tomoro...reson i cry
cause you been so good to me mr wigin an nobody aint never been
that good to me an make me think im somebody."[54] Thus,
Jefferson's achievement of his manhood, his acceptance of his
fate, and his ability to reason seem parallel. But when read in
conversation with the final section of *Native Son*, Gaines's
mockery of the Enlightenment and of the second significant
element of the "Jefferson's Diary" section of the novel becomes
apparent. Self-expression, not reasoning, as the Enlightenment
purports, becomes the distinctive feature of humanity.[55]

While the lateness of Jefferson's acquisition of this ability
has an obvious visible effect on his life, Bigger's inability to

---

[52]Ibid., 228.

[53]Ibid., 231.

[54]Ibid., 232.

[55]I reached many of the conclusions I assert here about Gaines's rewriting
of Wright's text and both authors' use of self-expression as an assertion of
humanity through conversations with Thinkwell Ngwenya. I thank him for this
contribution.

express himself frequently or meaningfully is in many ways his tragic flaw. But to a large degree, he lacks control of this ability because society refuses to acknowledge his attempts to express himself until he has committed two acts of murder. By then, his death is inevitable. Like Bigger, Jefferson recognizes (even if only unconsciously) the connections between self-expression and humanity. Thus, he refuses to talk at any length after being likened to a hog. But when he does begin to express himself, even at a most basic level (which, again, mocks the Enlightenment's tendencies toward erudition), his humanity cannot be legitimately denied or even questioned. Thus, Jefferson is not only able to accept his fate and walk to the chair like a man, but he also inspires Grant to accept his responsibility to the community and empowers that same community by proving that he is as much a man as those who ultimately kill him.

The recurring trope of confinement in contemporary African-American literature offers insight into the consequences of being denied freedom in a world that claims to offer freedom as an inalienable right. Ironically and unfortunately, many of these confined characters are not all that different from characters who are not physically or literally confined but who are no less imprisoned than those protagonists who can be accurately defined as confined characters-in-process. But unlike those texts in which the protagonist struggles, more or less in figurative freedom, to exist in a society that denies his humanity, texts that adopt and revise the trope of confinement allow us as readers to see the denial of mobility literally and perhaps then to imagine how a similar but figurative denial precedes physical confinement. Making this connection may just be one great lesson before dying.

Works Cited and Consulted

Boyd, Melba J. "Literacy and the Liberation of Bigger Thomas." In *Approaches to Teaching Wright's* Native Son, edited by James A. Miller, 35–41. New York: MLA of America, 1997.

Clark, Keith. *Black Manhood in James Baldwin, Ernest J. Gaines, and August Wilson*. Urbana: University of Illinois Press, 2002.

Ellison, Ralph. *Invisible Man*. 1952. Reprint, New York: Vintage, 1972.

Folks, Jeffrey J. "Communal Responsibility in Ernest J. Gaines's *A Lesson Before Dying*." *Mississippi Quarterly* 52/2 (Spring 1999): 259–71.

Forrest, Leon. *The Bloodworth Orphans*. New York: Random House, 1977.

————. *The Furious Voice for Freedom: Essays on Life*. Wakefield RI: Asphodel, 1994.

Gaines, Ernest. *A Lesson before Dying*. 1993. Reprint, New York: Vintage, 1994.

Gates, Henry L., Jr. *The Signifying Monkey: A Theory of African-American Literary Criticism*. New York: Oxford University Press, 1988.

Gaudet, Marcia, Ernest J. Gaines, and Reggie Young, editors. *Mozart and Leadbelly: Stories and Essays*. New York: Knopf, 2005.

Jablon, Madelyn. *Black Metafiction: Self-Consciousness in African American Literature*. Iowa City: University of Iowa Press, 1997.

Kearns, Edward. "The 'Fate' Section of *Native Son*." *Contemporary Literature* 12/2 (Spring 1971): 146–55.

Lee, A. Robert. "Sight and Mask: Ralph Ellison's *Invisible Man*." *Negro American Literature Forum* 4/1 (March 1970): 22–33.

Lowe, John. *Conversations with Ernest Gaines.* Jackson: University Press of Mississippi, 1995.

Miller, James A. "Bigger Thomas's Quest for Voice and Audience in Richard Wright's *Native Son.*" *Callaloo* 28/3 (Summer 1986): 501–506.

Mumford, Lewis. *The Golden Day: A Study of American Experience and Culture.* New York: Boni and Liveright, 1926.

Nash, William R. "'You Think a Man Can't Kneel and Stand?': Ernest J. Gaines's Reassessment of Religion as Positive Communal Influence in *A Lesson Before Dying.*" *Callaloo* 24/1 (Winter 2001): 346–62.

Winther, Per. "Imagery of Imprisonment in Ralph Ellison's *Invisible Man.*" *Black American Literature Forum* 17/3 (Autumn 1983): 115–19.

Wright, Richard. *Native Son.* 1940. Reprint, New York: HarperPerennnial, 1993.

Mind-Blown:
Possibility and Trauma in *Native Son*

Terry Bozeman

He who is educated by possibility is educated in accordance with his infinity. Possibility is therefore the heaviest of all categories.... When such a person, therefore goes out from the school of possibility and knows more thoroughly than a child knows the alphabet that he can demand of life absolutely nothing, and that terror, perdition, annihilation dwell next door to every man, and has learned the profitable lesson that even dread which alarms may the next instant become affect, he will interpret reality differently, he will extol reality, and even when it rests upon him heavily he will remember that after all it is far, far lighter than the possibility was.

—Søren Kierkegard[1]

Confidence could only come again now through action so violent that it would make him forget. These were the rhythms of his life: indifference and violence; periods of abstract brooding and periods of intense desire; moments

---

[1]Søren Kierkegaard, *The Concept of Anxiety: A Simple Psychologically Orienting Deliberation on the Dogmatic Issue of Hereditary Sin*, trans. Reidar Thomte (Princeton: Princeton University Press, 1980) 156.

of silence and moments of anger—like water ebbing and
flowing from the tug of a far-away, invisible force.

—*Native Son*[2]

I didn't want to kill! But what I killed for, I *am*!

—Bigger Thomas[3]

Houston Baker, Jr., aptly describes the world that gave birth to
Richard Wright as a place where "violence was omnipresent:
there were beatings by whites, black women raped, black men
fighting back as 'bad niggers,' black men castrated and lynched."[4]
Baker goes on to state that the mental and physical conditioning
of the persons under such stresses inculcates a primary existence
of a "survival motion" in life.[5] This survival motion Baker
discusses represents the day-to-day reality of life in the throes of
potential violence that one is unable to control. Rather than the
normality of occasional generic violence, those born into what
Margaret Walker in *Daemonic Genius* characterizes as a "cauldron
of pure hell" exist under levels of violence so heinous that it
often defies human logic and rationality.[6] It is this "motion" that
America impresses upon men like Bigger Thomas through
denying them their humanity and a sense of subjectivity that
confines them in a living hell.

While reading *Native Son*, Harold Bloom, like many,
rationalizes that one should fear Bigger Thomas. Standing on the
edge of paranoia, created by America, Bigger represents the

---

[2]Richard Wright, *Native Son* (New York: Harper Perennial–Harper-
Collins, 1993) 31.

[3]Ibid., 501.

[4]Houston Baker, Jr., ed., *Twentieth Century Interpretations of Native Son*
(Englewood Cliffs NJ: Prentice Hall, 1972) 2.

[5]Ibid., 2.

[6]Margaret Walker, *Richard Wright, Daemonic Genius* (New York: Harper
and Row, 1988) 3.

ultimate manifestation of what Bloom labels as an "authentic bogeyman."[7] However, this personified monster, rather than be content to exist on the periphery of the American consciousness, stands and emits a "long thin song of defiance" at those who force him into a cornered existence.[8] And like the rat that he crushes in the opening scene of the novel, Bigger too suffers because of the fact of his birth and the accompanying "motions" of his existence underscore his position as pariah in the world. His mother articulates this when she declares, "Bigger, sometimes I wonder why I birthed you."[9] In fact, Bigger's own mother articulates another thought readers have asked of Bigger Thomas: "Boy, sometimes I wonder what makes you act like you do," as if he can even articulate those reasons himself. Her questioning his existence and why he "acts" like he does, when examined in light of criticism, are perhaps why scholars, nearly six decades after the novel's publication, continue to examine Bigger Thomas. There ultimately has to be an understanding of *how* Bigger Thomas lived—of his "survival motion"—so that his death has meaning. Yet, before critiquing how Bigger Thomas lived, we must try to understand why he lived the way he did. I argue that Wright uses the theories of Kierkegaard to frame Bigger as a character.

One fundamental in the rationale of this argument is that readers are compelled to see Bigger as he sees himself in the novel. Bigger sees himself early on in the novel as someone trapped in a life without hope, without feelings of joy, and quite simply without possibility of anything other than acute stagnancy. Kierkegaard, in much of *The Concept of Dread*, lays out the importance of this type of outlook on the individual psyche of persons limited by the concomitant lack of possibility in their

---

[7]Harold Bloom, ed., *Bigger Thomas* (New York: Chelsea House, 1990) 5.
[8]Wright, *Native Son*, 4.
[9]Ibid., 6.

lives. In fact, Bigger feels "ensnared in a tangle of deep shadows as black as the night that stretched above his head."[10] Clearly, the question of why he lived the way he did is shaped by the perception of his place in life.

One important fact to note however, according to Wright biographer Hazel Rowley, is that Wright did not read Kierke-gaard's *The Concept of Dread* until 1947, well after the publication of *Native Son*.[11] However, Kierkegaard's conceptualization of dread in Wright's formulation of Bigger is undeniable. In sum-mary, Kierkegaard's *The Concept of Anxiety: A Simple Psychologically Orienting Deliberation on the Dogmatic Issue of Hereditary Sin* raises important concerns that address Wright's assertion that the individual has to seek his own sense of freedom within society by confronting and embracing his own subjectivity. As Kierkegaard philosophizes on the issue of subjectivity, he argues that Man, since the fall of Adam, is forever guided by the ultimate manifestations of "nothingness." This represents the ultimate voiding of an individual's autonomy. Thus, by framing *Native Son* as a text into a Kierkegaardian paradigm of dread, one is able to fully acknowledge the power of possibility denied in manhood as an act of confinement in Bigger's life. Once placed within the framework of Kierkegaardian theory, *Native Son* and Bigger Thomas can be more fully appreciated. Specifically, through reading Bigger Thomas through this lens one gets clarity on how Bigger's life is guided by his lack of possibility, his com-prehension of his infinity, and ultimately his fear of annihilation.

First and foremost, "possibility" is the potential to achieve and go from nothing to a position of something. It is the ability to be one who, if given the chance promised in the very fabric of American ideology, pulls himself up by the bootstraps. But,

---

[10]Ibid., 82.

[11]Hazel Rowley, *Richard Wright: The Life and Times* (New York: Henry Holt, 2001) 357.

unfortunately for men like Bigger, it's often difficult if not impossible to pull on straps that don't exist in the first place. Thus when readers meet Bigger, he has already internalized the denials of "possibility" fully in accordance with his socially constructed "infinity" and therefore his understanding of "nothingness" is that he will never hope to have anything in his life that is of consequence. Once he has come to acknowledge the possibilities in his life, Bigger knows that his position is finite and without hope. Therefore, he struggles against annihilation even before he can live.

Wright's examination of Bigger's sense of dread—what he terms in "How Bigger Was Born" as "the Bigger Thomas conditioning"[12]—initiates the action of the novel. Placed in the position of the family's provider, Bigger finds himself deeply conflicted and constricted by his inability to either accept or reject the role of provider. Though he does not rejoice in his position as the family's provider and protector, Bigger internalizes his position at the beginning of the novel as a denial of his personal possibilities, which should not be taken lightly. One should not be so presumptive to say that perhaps Bigger should just grow up and be a man; that's the very problem he is faced with. As he rids the kitchenette of his family's immediate threat—the large black rat—Bigger acts out his own frustrations of being cornered in a life without the possibility of ever being a man. While the rat itself represents a physical concern for the family, in this scene it is the psychological and emotional threat represented that must be destroyed. For Bigger, the rat represents his frustrations. Specifically, it reminds him of the unending shame and pent-up rage in his life. The daily humiliation of poverty forces him to turn his head and gaze "into a far corner of the room"[13] and assume the responsibility as man

---

[12]Wright, *Native Son and "How 'Bigger' Was Born,"* 513.
[13]Ibid., 1.

of the house. Yet as the man of the house he can't keep the rats out. This position places the reality of his family's impending starvation and continued degradation squarely on his shoulders, which are already burdened with the impossibility of ever making a decision for and about himself. Nevertheless, before the decision is made for him, Bigger gets caught up in a level of neurosis that he feels he cannot control. He rejects being forced to be a man in the eyes of everyone but himself, which stresses him more. In fact, like the child referenced in the above quote by Kierkegaard, Bigger "knows he can demand of life absolutely nothing" at this point.[14]

To his family, he cannot be a man without a job. For Bigger, the idea of manhood exists in his desire to make decisions for himself and have them respected by others as the result of something that he has chosen. As a result, his sense of self-consciousness is primarily the ability to obtain, based on the amount of power allowed to him as an individual socially, economically, and spiritually, a sense of individualized actualization of his existence. This is his subjectivity; this should be his manhood. As a consequence of his frustration, Bigger reacts in ways that many readers find disturbing. His initial act of manhood—killing the rat—proves to be so irrational that it warrants a closer examination. While on the surface, Bigger's extermination of the rat seems an appropriate thing to do at the moment, the situation quickly deteriorates into a state of mayhem in which Bigger takes particular delight. To begin with, once the rat is dead Bigger still feels compelled to take a shoe and violently crush the rat's head. It's as if the death of the rat was not enough; it (the rat) had to receive additional destruction to allow Bigger his moment of catharsis. Further, the way in which Bigger uses the dead rat to terrorize his sister only masks the reality he hides deep within:

---

[14]Kierkegaard, *The Concept of Anxiety*, 156.

"He knew that the moment he allowed himself to feel its fullness how they lived, the shame and misery of their lives, he would be swept out of himself with fear and despair. So he held toward them an attitude of iron reserve; he lived with them, but behind a wall, a curtain. He knew that the moment he allowed what his life meant to enter fully into his consciousness, he would either kill himself or someone else. So he denied himself and acted tough."[15] The problem with Bigger's means of existing within his frustrated life is that he is always reactionary. Like the black rat he has killed, Bigger too lives simply guided by reflex motions and is himself punished for being what he is in the world.

Bigger's response, therefore, is to engage in a "survival motion" that forces him to react to his society according to what he fears would be the automatic consequences of his each and every action. Therefore, like the rat, Bigger seeks to avoid being cornered. He knows that his death would come at a terrible price greater than his death. To some, these reactions seem highly irrational. These responsive motions all manifest out of the negation of his sense of a distinct self grounded in the denial of any possibilities in his life. Yet because he has lived a life filled with death, Bigger kills because he wants to live as a free man with possibilities. The fact that he kills underscores Bigger's reactionary responses as and within his survival motion. In fact, these violent responses offer him possibility. For example, at the moment where Bigger struggles with himself before deciding to rob Blum's delicatessen early in the novel, there is evidence of how violence guides his life and takes him to the edge of possibility. Tortured by his own fears, Bigger's defense against admitting his own fear encases itself in violence. Though he could have called off the robbery, Bigger hoped that Gus's refusal

---

[15]Wright, *Native Son and "How 'Bigger' Was Born,"* 9.

would be enough to end it all and not reveal his own fears. At this moment, "he hated Gus because he knew that Gus was afraid, as even he was; and he feared Gus because he felt that Gus would consent and then he would be compelled to go through with the robbery."[16] Here the possibility is that through an act of violence (Bigger's assault on Gus) the robbery would not take place. However, there are more revealing looks at Bigger's need for violence as a way of expression. Subsequent scenes reveal how truly distressed Bigger is at the moment. He wonders to himself how it would feel to "hit Gus squarely in the mouth," or to stab him.[17] But these thoughts of violence are held in check inside his own community, inside his own mind. Yet, because his acts of violence are contained within the Southside, they have no meaning for his life other than as an exercise to his frustrations. However, once this release begins outside his own neighborhood and the accidental killing of Mary Dalton takes place, Bigger can now situate himself as the catalyst of other's reactions on a larger more meaningful scale; he establishes his subjectivity through violence. This subjectivity is ultimately his prison because there is no quantifiable way to balance this equation: "Confidence could only come again now through action so violent that it would make him forget. These were the rhythms of his life: indifference and violence; periods of abstract brooding and periods of intense desire; moments of silence and moments of anger—like water ebbing and flowing from the tug of a far-away invisible force."[18] Seeking the possibilities that come with his subjectivity causes Bigger at the same time to negate others. In a sense then, Bigger exists as both victim and victimizer. As victim, he is pushed by the unending imbalance of possibility in his life. Because he is victimized, Bigger acts out his frustrations both consciously and

---

[16]Ibid., 27.
[17]Ibid., 27–28.
[18]Ibid., 31.

otherwise against those around him. Yet because the subtext of Bigger's murder of Mary Dalton and the subsequent hunt for him is precluded by the idea that he may have raped her as well, it takes center stage in the novel. Laura Tanner's *Intimate Violence* makes an excellent point concerning how violence can allow an individual to work through the construction of his subjectivity. She argues that "for the violator, violence may come to serve as a temporary affirmation of an unstable self, a material manifestation of a disembodied ideology, an expansion of one's own insubstantial form out into an alien world. For the victim, however, violence is defined by a literal and psychological destruction of form, a threat to personal coherence, a sacrifice of self-control."[19] This comes to represent how Bigger's reactions allow him to rationalize his life. It is with this ability to rationalize one's position as a subject in the relationships of life that the individualized identity of self is born within Bigger Thomas. Bigger's desire for this "self" anchors in the idea that he wants to be a man in the reality of white society. In his own thoughts, Bigger wants "to be an idea" in "their minds"[20] that they respect. He wants also for this to be something that his mother respects as well. Yet for him and "his kind" as the novel relates, "they were a sort of a great natural force, like a stormy sky looming overhead, or like a deep swirling river stretching suddenly at one's feet in the dark,"[21] which prohibits him from being a man.

In Bigger's understanding, to be a complete "idea," that is, a "man"—more specifically what Roy Martinez in *Kierkegaard and the Art of Irony* terms the "single individual" (*den Enkelte*)[22]—

---

[19]Laura E. Tanner, *Intimate Violence: Reading Rape and Torture in Twentieth-Century Fiction* (Bloomington: Indiana University Press, 1994) 4.

[20]Wright, *Native Son and "How 'Bigger' Was Born,"* 147.

[21]Ibid., 129.

[22]Roy Martinez, *Kierkegaard and the Art of Irony* (Amherst NY: Humanity Books, 2001) 101.

seems for Bigger to be nothing more than having the ability to
choose, in whatever limited capacity, a path in life and to
acknowledge and have acknowledged by others its being a decision
as such. This represents Bigger's greatest level of understanding
within Kierkegaarad's paradigm of possibility. For Bigger, such an
actualization gives meaning to the question he asks Gus. Bigger
poses the question, "What in hell can a man do?"[23] but until he
understands his own sense of "being" in the context of being a
"man," Bigger will always be destined to bear the answer of
"nothing." Later, in his conversations with his lawyer, Max,
Bigger again tries to understand this "nothing" that comes with a
lack of possibility in his life. To Max's question on what he
wanted to do, Bigger responds, "nothing, I reckon. Nothing. But
I wanted to do what other people do."[24] For Bigger, to do
"nothing" should be a choice. He simply wants to have choices
in his life that are actually choices. In other words, Bigger simply
wants the possibilities to be there.

According to Merold Westphal's reading of Kierkegaardian
theory in *Becoming a Self: A Reading of Kierkegaard's Concluding
Unscientific Postscript*, "every human person [should be]
'something of a subject...a so-called subject of sorts.' Every day
[he should] make decisions that give content to [his] life."[25]
Westphal points out that making such decisions gives an
individual real, if only limited, *self*ness. If Bigger were able to see
himself as a speaking "subject" and not a spoken about "object,"
the beginnings of his manhood would be in place. Such an act
represents "freedom's first possibility."[26] Without this sense of
self-awareness, Bigger could have never been free in society.

---

[23]Wright, *Native Son and "How 'Bigger' Was Born,"* 22.
[24]Ibid., 408; emphasis added.
[25]Merold Westphal, *Becoming a Self: A Reading of Kierkegaard's Concluding
Unscientific Postscript* (West Lafayette IN: Purdue University Press, 1996) 101.
[26]Ibid., 102.

Each day would have continued to be that day of possible "annihilation" that Kierkegaard discusses.[27] Again, with the possibility to do something with his life, "nothing" may not have been such a terrible option for him.

Consequently, understanding the rationalization of "possibility" as a countering mechanism to his feeling of annihilation offers a way of examining and understanding the socio-psychological intricacies existent in Bigger's life. Focusing on the issue of possibility and subjectivity allows one to witness the other side of pathological symptoms in the mental and physical conditioning of Bigger Thomas as he seeks to achieve conscious perception of his "Self" with some basic possibilities in his life. Most important, the focus on Bigger's search to give voice and meaning to the individual "I" of his life reveals his desires to be something other than the metaphorical black rat in America. As long as Bigger lives as that rat in society, everywhere he turns there will be signs that reinforce the sentiment "YOU CAN'T WIN."[28] What the signs represent is that so long as Bigger believes and everything around him supports the idea, complete and total annihilation remains an ever-present danger in his life.

In his understanding of survival, Bigger feels he kills in self-defense (in the physical sense) and in Self-defense (in protecting a self-acknowledged being). For example, Mary's death results from his reaction to the "possibility" of being exposed for transgressing one of America's most unforgiving of taboos. Though he only carries Mary, who is too drunk to walk, to her room, the fact remains that he is black and she is white. To overlook the connotations of such an act—a black man and a white woman together, alone, in a bedroom in 1940 in America—is to be naïve to Bigger's reality. When Mrs. Dalton enters the room,

---

[27]Ibid., 156.
[28]Wright, *Native Son and "How 'Bigger' Was Born,"* 13.

Bigger's understanding of having transgressed a sacred law becomes his rationalized center. The "possibility" of an explanation never even materializes for Bigger. All he can know at that moment "was that they kill us for women like her."[29] That is a situation that can offer no possible options. As a matter of fact, once Mary is dead, life becomes real for Bigger: "The reality of the room fell from him; the vast city of white people that sprawled outside took its place. She was dead and he had killed her. He was a murderer, a Negro murderer, a black murderer. He had killed a white woman."[30] It is important to note that Bigger's thoughts at this moment are clearly articulated in terms of black and white. Note that he is clear in his thoughts that he is black like the rat and therefore will be dealt with accordingly.

Such factors severely hinder Bigger's ability to rationalize. A series of dichotomous relationships spiral him uncontrollably towards his fate; Bigger's perception of Mrs. Dalton testifies to this. Bigger's first thought of Mrs. Dalton is to note that she has a "face and hair that were completely white. She seemed to him a ghost."[31] For Bigger, being in the presence of Mrs. Dalton is to feel the all-knowing eye of God. In his every step and thought he feels that she senses him,[32] much like the all-seeing eye of the district attorney, Mr. Buckley, and the all-seeing eye of God. If Bigger were able to separate himself from the stresses of his lack of possibilities, he may have been able to save his own life. In his sense of reality, however, he must come to understand that the law of men will enact final judgment, damnation, and death, only to be followed by God's law and final judgment, damnation, and

---

[29]Ibid., 405.
[30]Ibid., 100.
[31]Ibid., 52.
[32]Ibid., 68.

eternal hell. The psychology inherent in this line of thought forces him into a continuous state of chaos.

In his inability to fully separate the law (the earthbound god) from the spiritual God, inside his head, Bigger demands clarity. Therefore, we have a partial explanation of why each and every act of violence committed by Bigger occurs to the head of the victim. There appears to be a need to destroy, or at best control the part of the victim that is the center of his own sense of powerlessness. It is no accident that Bigger crushes the skulls of the rat and of Bessie, severs the head of Mary, and places the knife at Gus's throat as a proliferation of his own sense of power. Bigger seems to be symbolically voicing a need for someone to understand the demons inside his head. One may also read these scenes to show that Bigger may be trying to separate himself from them.

Nevertheless, a sympathetic examination of Bigger does not attempt to remove the fact of the actual violence committed by Bigger; instead, it allows an exploration of the mitigating circumstances of his desire to exist subjectively in an objective manner. By doing this, instead of categorizing Bigger as that authentic American monster, one can see that there may be a hint of complexity to Bigger Thomas other than as a flat dimensionless character. But, as Max tries to explain to the court later in the novel, one has to examine Bigger as a three-dimensional figure to appreciate his situation. Max argues before the court that there needs to be some exploration of Bigger's motives behind these murders. He even suggests that "murder" may not be the best way to examine the deaths of Mary and Bessie because they lack motive.

> The truth is, Your Honor, there is no motive as you and I understand motives within the scope of our laws today. The truth is, this boy did *not* kill! Oh, yes; Mary Dalton is

dead. Bigger Thomas smothered her to death. Bessie
Mears is dead. Bigger Thomas battered her with a brick in
an abandoned building. But did he murder? Did he kill?
Listen: what Bigger Thomas did early that Sunday
morning in the Dalton home and what he did that Sunday
night in that empty building was but a tiny aspect of what
he had been doing all his life long! He was *living*, only as
he knew how, and as we have forced him to live. The
actions that resulted in the death of those two women
were as instinctive and inevitable as breathing or blinking
one's eyes. It was an act of *creation!* [33]

Max indicates that the inevitability of Bigger's path to
destruction has been marked by the denial of possibility
throughout his life. But one still has to ponder how those deaths
are acts of "creation." The possibility of creation is what Bigger
has been denied all his life. Instead of thinking he can choose to
become something or someone, Bigger has his life prescribed to
him. In his defense of Bigger, Max attempts to articulate this
negated possibility of creation in terms of Bigger's reality. He
argues before the court that Bigger "attended school where he
was taught what every white child was taught; but the moment he
went through the door of the school into life he knew that the
white boy went one way and he went another."[34] For Bigger,
school itself represents a further denial of possibility. It offers no
closer understanding of the freedoms of America; it only
highlights the inconsistencies and stifles him into deeper sense
of confinement within the reality that he can never create a life
for himself.

Another way of understanding Bigger's sense of confinement
requires an interrogation of other ways in which he is severely

---

[33]Ibid., 466.
[34]Ibid., 458.

confined by unattainable possibility. In Bigger's case, he is also expressly confined by his inability to interact meaningfully with his family. He feels that his family, his link to humanity, plays a role in the negation of his Self. In this situation, for him, family and friends come to represent elements of black society who use religion and other forms of passive resistance as numbing mechanisms. By viewing others in this light, Bigger places himself on the outside of the community. He can't reach out to them because they too lack the self-awareness necessary to express a desire for the possibilities inherent in being in America. Thus it happens that the environment and key situations conspire to create within Bigger what Jerry Bryant terms a "compliant nullity."[35] This strife within his interior family relationships disallows Bigger from meaningfully connecting with anyone. He needs this support and understanding but can't get it because he is not like them. As a matter of fact, the one scene in the entire novel where a family member actually tries to speak up for Bigger is short-lived, though very important. When Bigger's brother Buddy tries to speak on his behalf over breakfast, his mother quickly tells him to shut up or "get up from this table."[36] Mrs. Thomas feels that Bigger should be glad to get the job at the Dalton home. Bigger is not. He responds, "What you want me to do? Shout?"[37] This signifies a powerful statement that Bigger makes towards his mother and how she copes with life through the church. In this scene, the question of whether or not he should shout makes a mockery of religious submission and graciousness at receiving the scraps from America's bounty. It also represents Bigger's attempt at articulating his need to yell out in protest. But again this comes at a severe price for Bigger.

---

[35]Jerry Bryant, *Victims and Heroes: Racial Violence in the African American Novel* (Amherst: University of Massachusetts Press, 1997) 203.
[36]Wright, *Native Son and "How 'Bigger' Was Born,"* 10.
[37]Ibid., 12.

Subsequently, Bigger further suffers from his refusal to see hope and the possibilities in religion of the type his mother represents. Since he cannot live by the laws of the Christian church, he lives at odds with his family and the white world. As long as he does not submit to religion and the inherent stereotypical passivity, the potential eruption of his revolt against the world around him looms about. Such a potential threat cannot be tolerated. In situations where there is not a total rejection of the church, Bigger seems at war within himself. In her article "Richard Wright: Climate of Fear and Violence," Obioma Nnaemeka writes that Bigger realizes his mother's Christian religion has its promises and attractions, but he psychologically rejects the religion because he cannot accept its demands.[38] The concept of religion does not allow Bigger the space needed to assert a sense of individuality; in his case it denies him possibility. Bigger states that "it [religion] had a center, a core, an axis, a heart which he needed but could never have unless he laid his head upon a pillow of humility and gave up his hope of living in the world."[39] In order for him to realize the promises made by America, Bigger feels that he needs to be part of the world. Religion takes him out of the world; the promises of an afterlife have no meaning for him. Nnaemeka also states that Bigger finds the unity between religion and life on earth "shameful and futile."[40] He knows that he will never be fully accepted into society even if he does embrace religion. This aspect of his personal understanding of religion leads Bigger to treat everything around him as hostile to his existence. Ultimately, not being part of the church, for Bigger, increases these hostilities and furthers his sense of alienation. He would later note his antagonistic

---

[38]Obioma Nnaemeka, "Richard Wright: Climate of Fear and Violence," *The Western Journal of Black Studies* 16/1 (Spring 1992): 14–20.

[39]Wright, *Native Son and "How 'Bigger' Was Born,"* 294.

[40]Nnaemeka, "Climate of Fear and Violence," 18.

feelings toward the church. The disillusionment comes because of the central premise that "told him to bow down and ask for a mercy he knew he needed; but his pride would never let him do that, not this side of the grave, not while the sun shone."[41] Bigger knows that mercy does not exist for men like him. Therefore, he refuses to submit.

Bigger's sense of impending annihilation is heightened because in his world, there is little distinction between a white god—the men on earth who set the rules of existence and enforce the consequences of these rules—and the white God—the one who allows His earthly minions to oppress, set the rules of life and death, and enforce the consequences. For Bigger, both the mortal god and the eternal God prove jealous, and they both exact final vengeance via the threat of the day of judgment as a means for control. Bigger Thomas cannot recognize an either/or in this relationship and is therefore confined by the strict requirements of both; his rationalized observation of this power is total. For Bigger there is just God/god. In his world God/god solidifies the materialization of his oppressive existence. Everything he experiences results from this power-sharing plan. This inescapable plan leads Bigger to feel a sense of never-ending outside control. His understanding is that "they ruled him, even when they were far away and not thinking of him, ruled him by conditioning him in his relations to his own people."[42] Appropriately then, it is important to understand that all of Bigger's relations to any manifestation of God leave him completely restricted and choked off from possibility.

Martinez in "Kierkegaard and Otherness" discusses man's existence and his relationship to God, arguing that one's existence is "in the process of becoming, and every individual man...is or should be conscious of being in the process of

---

[41]Wright, *Native Son and "How 'Bigger' Was Born,"* 359–60.
[42]Ibid., 130.

becoming." He goes on to note that "for this reason life is to be lived in fear and trembling" because this response "signifies that a [God/god] exists."[43] In other words, for Bigger, the fact that he perpetually seeks to "become" something he can never really achieve chokes out of him any real sense of freedom. Through Bigger's rationalization, the hypocrisies of being a child of God/god stand in blatant relief to his life, evidenced in examples such as the one scene where Mrs. Thomas is singing the spirituals one minute and is telling him she wishes he wasn't born the next.[44] Bigger's feelings of suffocation highlight America's contradictions of him being a boy and a man, an adult and a child, a self and an "other" guided by that "tug of a far-away, invisible force."[45] For Bigger, God/god represents an emasculator, the negation of his manhood, and the negation of his Self. Yet in order to attain, not reclaim, the little he understands about manhood and break this feeling of confinement, Bigger feels that he only needs to make a decision of substance in his life and be able to stand up and say that it was his own decision. Instead, Bigger lives resigned to believing that "they [God/god] don't let us do nothing."[46] The choices he has before him are a job he can't refuse or starvation. Hand in hand, everything in Bigger's life, to this point, connects a god who tells him where to live, work, go and not go, to the God to whom his mother prays and sings. The frustration compounds for Bigger when his mother prays to God saying, "Lord, we thank Thee for the food You done placed before us for the nourishment of our bodies. Amen," but still in the same breath she says, "you going to have to learn to get up earlier than this, Bigger, to hold a job."[47] This angers

---

[43]Martinez, *Kierkegaard and the Art of Irony*, 104.
[44]Wright, *Native Son and "How 'Bigger' Was Born,"* 6.
[45]Ibid., 31.
[46]Ibid., 20.
[47]Ibid., 10.

Bigger because his mother thanks God for the food he (Bigger) must work to provide. For Bigger, religious passivity is an unacceptable outlook. Bigger belives it is ridiculous to work and not get any of the thanks for food he brings in. As a matter of fact, he would be even further humiliated by the fact that his own brother cannot speak in his defense at that very same table. Consequently, his process of trying to "become" someone chokes him by its boundaries.

Fundamentally, the boundaries that define Bigger's existence are the result of limited or nonexistent possibilities. The boundaries manifest in the form of walls. In the home, Bigger becomes accustomed to the strife and he wants out, but he has no options; whenever he asks himself what he can do to better his life, his mind hits a blank wall and he stops thinking.[48] Likewise, in one of the few moments when he tries to articulate himself when talking to one of his friends, Bigger's back is against a "red brick wall."[49] Standing on the street with Gus, Bigger tries to articulate his need to dream, his desire to try something, anything; his want for something to happen to him seems to drive him along in life. Here, Kierkegaard's idea of possibility and dread leads one to conclude that Bigger cannot function *because* he has the desire to dream, to fly, to "be," but ultimately realizes, "we the only things in this city that can't go where we want to go and do what we want to do."[50] Despite these desires, which seem to suggest the possibility of freedom, Bigger remains confined because he has not been given the tools to facilitate a belief that he can achieve these things as tangible possibilities in his life. Bigger recognizes that he was born into and will forever remain in a state of social confinement. Yet even with the pain of his possibilities being negated, Bigger cannot seek the comforts of

---

[48]Ibid., 12.
[49]Ibid., 15.
[50]Ibid., 22.

religion or alcohol because to do so would weaken him to the reality of his world. Having rejected these as coping strategies, Bigger leaves himself virtually defenseless. He feels and knows that he is being placed in a position to do something he cannot help.[51]

Regardless of how one reads Bigger Thomas, Wright's depiction of Bigger draws the ire of many critics because of the extreme violence in this novel. Exploring this violence ultimately advances the notion that Bigger should be seen as a protagonist who does attempt to reach out in limited ways towards establishing his subjectivity. But in a society that has conditioned him to be the "Big Nigger" that Kinnamon references, Bigger lives a life where he is forced to react that way. America created and conditioned Bigger to be this way by denying his humanity. While there ultimately must be some personal responsibility on his part as well, Bigger is never given the tools to engage society except as a threat. When Bigger reacts, he does just that; he reacts as a threat to that which threatens him. The nature of his existence demands that he survive, and survival remains the top priority. It no longer concerns him, to a certain point, that his existence runs contrary to the laws of society.

However, moving back to Bigger's position of dread, as Kierkegaard theorizes "he who becomes guilty through anxiety is indeed innocent, for it was not he himself but anxiety, a foreign power, that laid hold of him, a power that he did not love but about which he was anxious. And yet he is guilty, for he sank in anxiety, which he nevertheless loved even as he feared it."[52] A precise interpretation means that according to God/god's law, Bigger stands guilty as charged; however, if the world existed where might did not always equal right and everyone were truly equal and conscious of a self, Bigger would only be guilty by

---

[51]Ibid., 23.
[52]Kierkegaard, *The Concept of Anxiety*, 42.

reason of anxiety. Put another way, one cannot refuse to listen to Max's plea that we understand motive in Bigger's actions. Max argues forcefully: "He has no education. He is poor. He is Black. And you know what we have made those things mean in our country. I say I talked to him. Did I find ambition there? Yes. But it was blurred and hazy; with no notion of where it was to find an outlet. He knew he did not have a chance; he *believed it*. His ambition was chained, held back; a pool of stagnant water. Did he have the hope of a better life? Yes. But he kept it down, under rigid control."[53]

Nevertheless, it is this sense of anxiety that brings Bigger to his understanding of his existence. Facing the reality of his incarceration and the tangibility of his death, Bigger "would not mind dying now if he could only find out what this meant, what he was in relation to all the others that lived, and the earth upon which he stood."[54]

For him, after a life of confinement, it is the moment of actually being inside the steel and concrete cage that offers any meaning to his life, and he is able to see the realization of "possibility" before him. He has lived as an animal; what he needs in the end is to know how to die like a man[55] so that his time on earth comes to mean something. That meaning—that understanding of who or what he is—finally takes form in his own closing words and actions as he symbolically stands and embraces his "being" and accepts it in the words, "I ain't trying to forgive nobody and I ain't asking for nobody to forgive me. I ain't going to cry. They wouldn't let me live and I killed. Maybe it ain't fair to kill, and I reckon I really didn't want to kill. But when I think

---

[53]Wright, *Native Son and "How 'Bigger' Was Born,"* 470.
[54]Ibid., 420.
[55]Ibid., 495.

of why all the killing was, I begin to feel what I wanted, what I am."[56]

Through his final statement, Bigger momentarily leaves an opening for the reader to ponder Bigger's existence, proving that he has truly been reborn. One could read the comment to mean that Bigger accepts his socially imposed monster status. On the other hand, one should read it as Bigger's declaration of his subjectivity. It is a declaration that tests and tastes its fruition through the bars of his cell door as he calls out to Max to "tell Jan hello."[57] It is with his last contact with a human before the guards lead him to the death chair that Bigger, by not referring to Jan, a white man, as mister, speaks his position as a man who has grasped possibility and embraced it. In his last act, Bigger robs from those who would seek to harm him, their ability to fully annihilate him.

Works Cited

Baker, Houston, Jr., editor. *Twentieth Century Interpretations of Native Son*. Englewood Cliffs NJ: Prentice Hall, 1972.

Bloom, Harold, editor. *Bigger Thomas*. New York: Chelsea House, 1990.

Bryant, Jerry. *Victims and Heroes: Racial Violence in the African American Novel*. Amherst: University of Massachusetts Press, 1997.

Howe, Irving. "Black Boys and Native Sons." In *A World More Attractive*. New York: Horizon Press, 1963.

---

[56]Ibid., 500.
[57]Ibid., 502.

Kierkegaard, Soren. *The Concept of Anxiety: A Simple Psychologically Orienting Deliberation on the Dogmatic Issue of Hereditary Sin*. Translated by Reidar Thomte. Princeton NJ: Princeton University Press, 1980.

Kinnamon, Kenneth, editor. *New Essays on* Native Son. Cambridge: Cambridge University Press, 1990.

Martinez, Roy. *Kierkegaard and the Art of Irony*. Amherst NY: Humanity Books, 2001.

Nnaemeka, Obioma. "Richard Wright: Climate of Fear and Violence." *The Western Journal of Black Studies* 16/1 (Spring 1992): 14–20.

Rowley, Hazel. *Richard Wright: The Life and Times*. New York: Henry Holt and Co., 2001.

Tanner, Laura E. *Intimate Violence: Reading Rape and Torture in Twentieth-Century Fiction*. Bloomington: Indiana University Press, 1994.

Tate, Claudia. "Black Boy: Richard Wright's 'Tragic Sense of Life.'" *Black American Literature Forum* 10/4 (Winter 1976): 117–19.

Walker, Margaret. *Richard Wright, Daemonic Genius*. New York: Harper and Row, 1988.

Westphal, Merold. *Becoming a Self: A Reading of Kierkegaard's Concluding Unscientific Postscript*. West Lafayette IN: Purdue University Press, 1996.

Wright, Richard. *Native Son and "How 'Bigger' Was Born."* Introduction by Arnold Rampersad. New York: Harper Perennial–HarperCollins, 1993.

Part II

Confined Spaces and Places

Ernest J. Gaines's *A Lesson Before Dying*: Freedom in Confined Spaces

Katherine Daley and Carolyn M. Jones

We all know—at least intellectually—that we're going [to die]. The difference is being told, "Okay, it's tomorrow at 10 A.M." How do you react to that? How do you face it? That, it seems to me, is the ultimate test of life.[1]

—Ernest J. Gaines

[To be a man is to be r]esponsible to one's self and to one's world. To me, a man, a woman...is someone who loves mankind.[2]

—Ernest J. Gaines

The issues of what it means to be a man or woman, of how to "stand up" at the moment of testing and in the face of death, and of how to make that act of standing one for humanity dominate Ernest J. Gaines's *A Lesson before Dying*.[3] These perennial themes in Gaines's novels intersect, in this most recent work, with an examination of religion through the vehicle of Jefferson's

---

[1] www.randomhouse.com/vintage/gaines/bio.html.
[2] Reese Fuller, "Ernest J. Gaines Transcript," http://www.reesefuller. com/words/gaines1.html.
[3] Ernest J. Gaines, *A Lesson before Dying* (New York: Vintage Books, 1993).

diary. The diary is produced in the relationship between Jefferson and Grant and in the confinement of a plantation society in 1948, in a jail cell, and on an inner pilgrimage. The diary is testimony—the response to the trial and verdict that Jefferson is not allowed to make in the court—and it is an epistle, an individual witness and, ultimately, community lesson and canonical teaching. In *A Lesson before Dying*, through this epistle, Gaines shows us how an oppressed people may reposition themselves in relation to the structures of the "master narrative" by redefining the language of those structures. This redefinition, which is an act of freedom, is communicated from the borders of the system that destroys dignity and limits power, and in this novel, the language and symbols of Christianity are key elements in Gaines's writing of freedom in confined spaces.

Gaines's use of Christian myths and symbols is unorthodox. We want to argue that this is a story of faith that uses Christian symbols and myths as vehicles for communicating a set of social values—values that Gaines associates with manhood. Faith, for Gaines, is not only an internal orientation towards the "other"; it also consists, in keeping with the Catholic setting of the novel, of works, of the importance of action taken in the world for others. Faith, as Herman Beavers puts it in *Wrestling Angels into Song*, is performance.[4] Gaines's values suggest that commitment is confinement and that to be bound is to be free. Faith is the ability to stand—but, for Gaines, to stand as a full human being in the world. The temptation is to read Jefferson as an ascetic, but his confinement is not to take him out of the world, but rather to help him reengage it. Standing, for Gaines, means responsibility, striving,[5] and exhibiting grace under pressure. From his aunt and

---

[4]Herman Beavers, *Wrestling Angels into Song: The Fictions of Ernest J. Gaines and James Alan McPherson* (Philadelphia: University of Pennsylvania Press, 1995) 177.

[5]Fuller, "Ernest J. Gaines Transcript."

from Hemingway, Gaines came to understand what "dignity under pressure" and "survival with dignity" mean.[6] Standing—and in Lesson, the additional act of kneeling[7]—is done in a situation of oppression, of confinement. These acts call for integrity, reliability, strength, and determination[8]—all of which make one good and contribute to community.

Grant begins and ends the narrative with "I was there but I was not there."[9] This statement is key in Christian understanding. It is St. Paul who offers the notion of the absent witness as legitimate apostle. Paul's experience with the Risen Christ confers his power and authority in the early church. This theme of vision as authoritative experience informs Christianity, from Paul through Constantine to the Great Awakening, in which African-American slaves participated, and through every mystic and prophet, including Martin Luther King, Jr. To be there and not there, therefore, is a statement of faith; all Christians believe in something they do not witness directly: "Now faith is the substance [RSV: assurance] of things hoped for, the evidence [RSV: conviction] of things not seen" (Hebrews 11:1). We want to emphasize that Gaines's statement of faith is not a sign of his conversion or an act of proselytizing. In fact, Gaines says very little about religion. He has said this: "Well, I don't think religions solve anything. It's good to believe…. For you to survive, you must have something greater than what you are, whether it's religion or communism, or capitalism or something else, but it must be something above what you are. But as of right now, I

---

[6]Marcia Gaudet and Carl Wooton, *Porch Talk With Ernest Gaines: Conversations on the Writer's Craft* (Baton Rouge: Louisiana State University Press, 1990) 66.

[7]Suzanne W. Jones, "New Narratives of Southern Manhood: Race, Masculinity, and Closure in Ernest Gaines' Fiction," *Critical Survey* 9/2 (August 1997): 37.

[8]Gaudet and Wooton, *Porch Talk*, 71–72.

[9]Gaines, *A Lesson before Dying*, 3.

don't think orthodox religion has solved anybody's problems."[10]
Gaines is doing what African Americans under oppression have
always done. He is appropriating what is at hand—in this case,
Christian symbols—to tell a story about a particular community's
and a particular man's struggle for freedom and dignity. As Valerie
Babb tells us, this is central in all of Gaines's fiction:
"Maintaining dignity and self-esteem under negative
circumstances is a constant theme in Gaines' fiction, and any
consideration of race and history will be evoked through the
motives and experiences of individual men and women...Their
voices reverberate through his canon as their life experiences
become the music of his text."[11] Jefferson, in his diary from the
prison cell, is the climactic and integrative, transgressive and
transformative, subversive and spiritual voice in *A Lesson before
Dying*.

The Christian imagery of the novel is significant even as it is
signified upon: scapegoat become sacrifice, the importance of
witness, the communication of a lesson, and the writing of a text,
one with its own transformational power, delivered by an apostle
(in this case, Paul). Confinement, in the Christian sense, is
either a source of terror or, like the monk's cell,[12] the space of
freedom. Gaines, though not Catholic himself,[13] uses the
Catholic culture of South Louisiana to situate the action of the
novel. Though the novel's six-month action begins in October,

---

[10]John Lowe, ed., *Conversations with Ernest Gaines* (Jackson: University
Press of Mississippi, 1995) 51–52.

[11]Valerie Babb, *Ernest Gaines* (Boston: Twayne Publishers, 1991) 14.

[12]The monastic life was and is one of physical confinement, but in that
confinement, one seeks the freedom of the soul. As David Chidester writes in
Christianity: A Global History (San Francisco: HarperCollins, 2000), "the
contemplative life directed the mind and heart toward God" (165), and it
prepared the soul to enter heaven and to stand pure before God.

[13]Gaudet and Wooton, *Porch Talk*, 68.

after the sugar cane harvest,[14] its significant events take place during the Holy Season. Confined in this time frame, the novel makes a ritual movement from fall to higher innocence. The climactic events of the book—Jefferson's writing his diary, which is his performance of faith, and Paul's delivering it as an epistle to the community—have religious and historical echoes. In historical terms, the diary is a modern example of the African-American slave narrative,[15] ending not in physical freedom but in spiritual freedom. It echoes, in that sense, Frederick Douglass's *Narrative of the Life of Frederick Douglass, An American Slave* in its insistence on both standing as a man and standing for others, for dignity and community, as elements of true manhood. As a spiritual document, the diary, delivered by Paul to Grant, is the lesson that will be taught to a generation of children educated in the church-school. This means that the diary stands as a proof

---

[14]Karen Carmean, *Ernest J. Gaines: A Critical Companion* (Westport CT: Greenwood Press, 1998) 118.

[15]In stating this, we agree with Kimberly Rae Connor in *Imagining Grace: Liberating Theologies in the Slave Narrative Tradition* (Urbana: University of Illinois Press, 2000). Connor argues, along with critics like Paul Gilroy, that African-American cultural production is key to understanding black freedom. Connor particularly sees such production as having theological meaning:

> For more than a century, artists working within the slave narrative tradition have been drawing on imaginative, symbolic, and creative language expressed in a variety of modes that relates their own concrete conditions to the cause of liberation. They have been creating on the level of religious consciousness and producing new cultural forms by which to reveal the transformative potential of the creative process. Although performing and identifying themselves as artists, they are also perceiving and reflecting theologically on the world. Their experiential *testimonies*, when shaped by the imagination, become *textimonies* and are as authentic as any systematic theology in addressing issues pertinent to liberation. (4, emphasis added)

Connor continues: "My aim is to show the creative and potential link between cultural production and religious expression and to demonstrate that cultural production and religious expression are interconnected and dependent in ways that can move communities toward liberation because they foster a creative imagining of possibility" (4)

text of what Grant thinks at the end of the novel: "Only when the mind is free has the body a chance to be free."[16]

The diary is the point in the narrative at which Grant confines himself. His voice, his worries and his fears, dominate the narrative to that point. When the diary is offered, Grant steps back. He has been self-centered and self-obsessed. When he receives the diary, his focus shifts from self to "other"—to the community and to Jefferson. He records the diary; then, he records the positions of various members of the community. Karen Carmean argues that this narrative shift creates a more comprehensive view than would a single narrative angle, it delivers the impact of Jefferson's execution, and it avoids "stereotypical community responses on execution day."[17] Epistle, as we will call Jefferson's diary, generates—is followed by— witness. Everyone in the community is forced to witness, in one way or another, to Jefferson's death. The community, black and white, is confined in this moment and defined by this act. There is no innocence, Gaines suggests, but there is something else: a possibility for freedom in the confined space of Southern American society and a possibility for a new relation to self, other, and God made through the death of one. We are defined ultimately, Gaines suggests, not by our situations and not by the master narrative, but by how we respond. Grant recognizes the significance of this moment—a moment that brings the deadly power of the social to the private consciousness of all. He wonders, "What happens after today? Nothing will ever be the same after today."[18]

There are multiple and interlocking modes of confinement in the novel, and Jefferson, as we will see, addresses all of these in his diary. Indeed, white Southern society depended on

---

[16]Gaines, *A Lesson before Dying*, 251.
[17]Carmean, *Ernest J. Gaines: A Critical Companion*, 119.
[18]Gaines, *A Lesson before Dying*, 248.

confinement, the absence of freedom, to understand what it meant to be free. As Toni Morrison suggests in *Playing in the Dark: Whiteness and the Literary Imagination*, "Nothing highlighted freedom—if it did not in fact create it—like slavery."[19] The slave—and we would add, the African American in the Jim Crow South—was, Morrison adds, a meditation on human freedom and on terror.[20] This accounts for the underlying, even quiet, sense of violence in *A Lesson before Dying*; we are witnessing the violent workings of a system of oppression. The mechanisms of this system—either overt or covert—keep everyone in "place." Overt violence regulates by force, punishing offenders; covert violence forces self-regulation and offenders punish themselves. The definition of Jefferson as a hog is the central example of systemic violence in the novel; he must be made animal in order for the court either to free him (as harmless) or to define and contain him (as dangerous). He is defined so that the system can work.

Confinement, in its many manifestations, therefore defines, preserves, and maintains order in the South, in America. Jefferson and Grant are confined by a racist white and, in the case of Louisiana, Creole and caste-ordered society whose values they have internalized. This situation of internal and external oppression manifests itself in multiple modes of confinement. Everyone in the novel is bound in Southern hierarchy. In South Louisiana, that hierarchy is complicated by a caste system based on race—defined by degrees of creolization—gender, and class. The system leads to physical confinement—segregation in schools[21]—not just in terms of black and white, but also in terms

---

[19]Toni Morrison, *Playing in the Dark: Whiteness and the Literary Imagination* (Cambridge: Harvard University Press, 1992) 38.

[20]Ibid., 37.

[21]Philip Auger, "A Lesson about Manhood: Appropriating 'The Word' in Ernest Gaines' *A Lesson before Dying*," *Mississippi Quarterly* 52/2 (Spring 1995): 76.

of creole and Catholic or not—in housing, and in worship. Public places are not free spaces but are places of confinement, as are private homes. Grant is controlled in the space of Pichot's house and exercises a counter-control by refusing to sit, eat, and drink in the traditionally African-American space of the kitchen.[22] There is also confinement in language. Grant does not speak in the educated way that he knows, but rather manages his speech. Names also free and confine. Miss Emma and Jefferson, for example, are never called by their full names by the white characters in the novel. In this sense, Grant, as "Mr. Wiggins," and Rev. Ambrose are exceptions; as preacher and teacher, they are the most mobile members of the African-American community.

Within this system, exchange—obligation, responsibility, and gift-giving— greatly regulatest social obligation. One driving force of the narrative is its women. Henri Pichot's obligation to Miss Emma is one that she uses to demand a gift. Grant and Jefferson work out of this usually unacknowledged space of community, and as their relationship grows, they expose and, in the cell, create a space that is different from "the way the world works"—at least, for a short time. They also, in the most basic definition of religion as "binding" (religio), unbind and rebind beliefs and persons according to new priorities. In the novel, relationships around food, for example—when food is eaten (time), where (space) it is eaten, who offers it, and with whom it is eaten (community)—signify power. These relationships, as much as official structures of power, such as law, build, bind, and regulate a community. When these relationships are changed, as they are in the cell, the space of confinement, the communal web, at least, vibrates and, at most, may be rewoven. Since women control most of these "unofficial powers," they initiate the tug and, doing so, they help Grant and Jefferson to reorient

---

[22]Gaines, *A Lesson before Dying*, 45.

the web. Grant and Jefferson do the work, however, and finally, Jefferson works alone. Together, they undercut the hierarchy of the racist South.

In this novel, Gaines also defines freedom by confining us, binding us, not just in space, but in time—in the year 1945 as well as in the movement of the novel itself. There is, on the one hand, a sense of stasis and immobility. Grant asks when things will change, indicating the slow movement of change in the South. His waiting for Vivian's divorce also seems interminable. This sense of protracted time, of meaningless repetition, guides the first part of the novel, as Grant treats his forced connection to Jefferson as an obligation: something inflicted on him. He feels bound to this burden—a burden from which he believes he will receive nothing. This changes as he begins to see his action as responsibility and commitment, as an investment made out of the power of choice and out of response. Obligation, therefore, is a response to power. Responsibility is undertaken out of love.

Concurrently, urgency sets in. Jefferson's execution is to take place right after Holy Week, and the major action of the novel is set from Advent to Easter. As Jeffrey J. Folks argues, this location in time "introduces a meaningful annual cycle around which the local community organizes its life."[23] This location marks the action of the novel as an extended ritual. Clifford Geertz has called ritual the repetition that creates.[24] In ritual, confinement is necessary, in space, in time, and in regulation of the body. To have significance, to connect human beings to the sacred—"other," community, and self—that which is in space, Catherine Albanese tells us, must be performed perfectly in

---

[23]Jeffrey Folks, "Communal Responsibility in Ernest J. Gaines's *A Lesson before Dying*," *Mississippi Quarterly* 52/2 (Spring 1999): 265.

[24]Clifford Geertz, "Making Experiences, Authoring Selves" in *The Anthropology of Experience*, ed. E. M. Bruner and V. W. Turner (Urbana: University of Illinois Press, 1986) 380.

time. As such, this intense time of repetition of visits and words stands counter to and undoes the stasis of Grant's life. In Jefferson and Grant, we witness birth, death, and resurrection, a repetition and movement within particular boundaries that constructs freedom.

This freedom is not the fleeing that Grant, at first, desires. To flee is not to have any boundaries; such a situation is not human. It means a life without true contact with the other and without any form in which to express the self. Instead, it is the power to move—to stand and to kneel[25]—and the yielding to the other that makes freedom possible. These body movements are ritual ones, and ritual is ordered by liturgy. Their repetition generates change within the multiple confined spaces in which Jefferson is imprisoned and in which Grant, finally, chooses to remain but not as the slave he recognizes himself to be. He, too, becomes a free man.

The unlikely altar—the site of transformation—is the prison, particularly the jail cell. The confinement of the narrative itself to this space and to the time of the Holy Season creates an intersection between politics and religion. It emphasizes Gaines's understanding of creative or redemptive suffering, an understanding in line with that of Dr. Martin Luther King. Change comes at a price, Gaines tells Wolfgang Lepschy in an interview published in *MELUS*: "You do suffer; you have to suffer in order to make any changes, especially when you have something so ingrained as racism and over so many years, in order to have any change at all. And it has to begin with one person, and others will follow. It's usually one person that must be willing to pay a big price to make this change."[26] From the understanding that comes through creative suffering, one

---

[25]Jones, "New Narratives," 37.
[26]Wolfgang Lepschy, "A *MELUS* Interview: Ernest J. Gaines," *MELUS* 24/1 (Spring 1999): 7

becomes responsible for others and generates rootedness. Rootedness is a creative and committed confinement—a living for others that is true freedom. For Gaines, rootedness is the power to stay in place and generate the change that makes a future possible: "those are the ones that have made all the difference in the South, staying working there, living there, fighting, and dying. They are the ones."[27]

Jefferson never will leave—physically—prison, but he finds freedom. His, as we indicated, is a freedom/slave narrative, but not of the classical type. It is not a learned work, like that of Douglass.[28] Jefferson is writing to a sympathetic African-American audience, not a skeptical white one, and he is writing to—at first—a single person: Grant. Grant provides the frame; he tells Jefferson that he must do "a" work. Herman Beavers argues that this makes the diary collaborative, a co-authored text that acknowledges an audience.[29] We would qualify this by affirming the value of collaboration as indicative of community, but by arguing that a man must face death alone, and that Jefferson, even as he writes to Grant, does so. Carlyle V. Thompson remarks that Grant's name "conjures up the historical and liberatory significance of Ulysses S. Grant."[30] Grant is also the "grant." He bestows trust and belief. "Grant" comes from the Latin *credentare*: to make to believe—credo—or trust. He also becomes a principle of conveyance or transfer—exchange. Grant, echoing Gaines's own sense of religion[31]—thinks that the community "must believe." They must believe in something larger than the

---

[27]Ibid.

[28]Carlyle Thompson, in "Gaines' *A Lesson before Dying*," *CLA Journal* (March 2002) 308, makes the comparison, but without our qualifications. Thompson's article is an excellent source for examining the significance of names in the narrative.

[29]Beavers, *Wrestling Angels*, 177.

[30]Thompson, "Gaines' *A Lesson before Dying*," 286.

[31]Lowe, *Conversations with Gaines*, 52.

self. Finally, in contrast to the classical slave narrative, Jefferson's is unfiltered. He does not erase;[32] he only marks out what he wants to change, and he does not edit. In this work, therefore, we receive a true stream of consciousness that defines and we witness a true struggle to come to terms with self, other, and God.

Suzanne Jones tells us that "friend," "hero," "scapegoat," and "myth" are the key words that Grant uses with Jefferson, and all are redefined in the men's interactions and in the diary. As language is offered and altered, the cell, originally a place of isolation and suffering, becomes a space of pure human interaction: a space of hospitality, a meeting place. Though Grant tells Jefferson that he must give to others and though Jefferson does, Grant opens the way so that others give to Jefferson. Jefferson is like one of the desert fathers: all go to him,[33] and a space of reciprocity opens in the cell. Jefferson is the center of gift giving, to which we will turn in a moment. He becomes an unlikely point of organization of community coherence, a point at which language and place change.

Such transformation of language and signification on myth is consistent with the African-American religious tradition. The black church tradition, for example, transformed the Christian mythology that confined it into a mythology of freedom. The language of the myth remains the same; the control of interpretation makes a space for freedom. This leads to a creative use of story, of metaphor, that is the basis of a culture of resistance. For example, African Americans, from slavery to Martin Luther King's final speech, have utilized and transformed

---

[32]Gaines, *A Lesson before Dying*, 229.

[33]In the early church, those who chose a life of asceticism often went into remote and desolate places to practice their Christian life. The public was fascinated by them and often followed them into these remote places to learn what the ascetic had learned. See Chidester, *Christianity*, 116–20. It is interesting that this phenomenon of ascetic retreat began in Egypt and is an African contribution to Christianity.

the myth of the Exodus. Dwight Hopkins makes this argument in "Slave Theology in 'The Invisible Institution.'" Hopkins argues that the slaves, working orally with Biblical text they heard preached to them, linked Jesus, on whom their hopes for spiritual freedom centered, with Moses, who had delivered a people from physical bondage. Hopkins explains, "far from being a whimsical interpretation of the Bible, black folks' retro-projection of Jesus to Moses' days reflects an authentic and faithful reading of scripture. The slaves correctly followed the instructions from the prologue of John's gospel, which didactically states, 'In the beginning was the Word and the Word was with God.' If the Word, who is Jesus, existed in the beginning of time, then surely Jesus had the ability and the power to exhort Moses during the latter's time."[34]

Re-appropriation and remaking of space is another feature of the African-American religious tradition. Such action is in line with Martin Luther King's method of non-violent resistance, for example. Those who worked with King took over—physically but peacefully—the sites at which injustice had been done to them: buses, lunch counters, drug stores, streets, and prisons. This activity of transformation of language and of place creates spaces for freedom within the structures of, on the borders of, terror and oppression. The diary occupies such a free space.

In his diary, Jefferson "goes deep,"[35] to examine both self and other. In doing so, he evaluates the significance of "friend," "hero," "scapegoat," and "myth"—the words that Grant uses with him. His diary becomes, when it is passed on, a letter, an epistle. The letter—as in Seneca's letters, Rilke's *Letters to a Young Poet*, and King's "Letter from a Birmingham Jail"—is a

---

[34]Dwight Hopkins, "Slave Theology in the 'Invisible Institution,'" in *Cut Loose Your Stammering Tongue: Black Theology in the Slave Narratives,"* ed. Dwight Hopkins and George Cummings (Maryknoll NY: Orbis Press, 1998) 20.

[35]Gaines, *A Lesson before Dying*, 228.

form in which a position or idea is defined and explained in a situation of exchange. In such documents, the writer addresses a silent interlocutor. The questioning voice is absent, except as it is implied in the response of the writer. The New Testament epistles function in the same way. They are letters to a particular community or individual addressing a particular situation, set of issues, or problem. These letters are responses to a call. Many times the letter indicates that the response is the only power the writer has. One cannot control, often, one's circumstances but one can control one's response. This Stoic strain is present in Paul's New Testament epistles and in Southern Christianity. The epistle's particularity becomes, however, a source, for an expanding community. The voice of one—and many of the New Testament epistles were written from prison—becomes the voice for all.

Jefferson begins as a lone voice. He has been, until he and Grant begin their talks, friendless. In the letter he records memories of his past. His earliest memory is of the water cart.[36] This is the moment that haunts Jefferson. He speaks of it with Grant when Grant tells him that he must take up the cross.[37] The image of taking up the cross is one of suffering and sacrifice, of, as Catholic liturgy expresses it, the sacrifice of the victim who brings reconciliation. The memory of Jefferson at six and in charge of the water cart reveals the point at which Jefferson became a social being; it is his earliest conscious memory. He is a child but one with the responsibility of an adult. His first definition of self—as one who must bring food and water on time—is given to him. He is on his own, without, he feels, support from anyone. He is a scapegoat, expelled from childhood and from true community.

---

[36]Ibid., 227.
[37]Ibid., 224.

As he writes, he generates identity and community—a "new testament"[38] for a world of confinement, and the scapegoat is transformed into a self-sacrificing suffering servant. His redefinitions will go forward in his letter. Jefferson is no longer one who is acted upon—the scapegoat—but is an actor—one who makes a choice to become an integral part of community. Hospitality, given and received, is the sign of this shift. The gift, as in Marcel Mauss, requires action. Mauss reminds us that the gift involves the obligation to give, to receive, and to reciprocate.[39] Gifts carry power—the power of the giver—and generate power as they generate more giving. Such a process is not outside the structures of power. Jacques Derrida reminds us that hospitality, which involves welcoming the stranger, carries with it the possibility of hostility and, in the limitation of self of both guest and host that hospitality necessitates, the presence of tension.[40] Gifts and hospitality, therefore, carry and define identity and bestow or take away honor. The process of giving material objects is a social glue that indicates a spiritual energy. In participating in this exchange, Jefferson defines his own power and, thereby, gives the community a source of power upon which to draw, as he becomes a hero.

Grant's pedagogy[41] generates hospitality: eating and sharing food, the giving of gifts (like the radio, which is paid for, partly, by the community), and the receipt of gifts (the letter). In this

---

[38]See Auger, "A Lesson about Manhood," 82. While we agree with the tenor of Auger's argument, we do not want to interpret the Christian themes as literally as he does—for example, to make Jefferson the "new Christ" (84). Auger makes a similar reading of the character of Paul (83–84), comparing him to St. Paul and arguing that Gaines's characterization "seems to fit almost too neatly" (83).

[39]Marcel Mauss, *The Gift: The Form and Reason for Exchange in Archaic Societies*, trans. W. D. Halls (New York: W. W. Norton, 1990) 39.

[40]John D. Caputo, *Deconstruction in a Nutshell: A Conversation with Jacques Derrida* (New York: Fordham University Press, 1997) 110.

[41]Jones, "New Narratives," 31.

exchange, Jefferson contemplates and redefines "friend," "hero," "scapegoat," and "myth." Heroism, the notion of the conquering individual whom the community carries on its shoulders, becomes the suffering servant, one who carries the burden of the community on his shoulders.

Heroism has less to do with power than it has to do with responsibility, the essence of manhood, for Gaines. He tells John Lowe that "I think we think that being a big tough guy...is being a man...that isn't what makes a man...this is the responsibility of man; taking responsibility for the whole, all humanity, is what I think manliness is."[42] Jefferson takes responsibility and accepts his role as the suffering servant who understands his suffering as part of his chosen state so that it becomes a task, not an outcome of oppression. Suffering, as Viktor Frankl reminds us in *Man's Search for Meaning*, is constitutive of existence: without suffering, there is no meaning and there is no true love.[43] In the acceptance of suffering, scapegoat becomes sacrifice. As scapegoat, Jefferson is without choice: he is a sign of terror and of what happens when one crosses boundaries. As sacrifice, he gives himself, and he, too, can receive. He can feel his godmother's love for the first time; he is not on his own. This sign of choice means that he becomes the opposite of the boy who, being dragged to the chair, called on Joe Louis[44] to save him. Jefferson walks.

All this emerges from his friendship with Grant, who is teacher and companion. A friend, according to Aristotle in the Nicomachean Ethics, is the "other self"—the one equal to you who can both love you and correct you. Friendship, therefore, teaches us to "other" the self. As such, friendship is the basis of

---

[42]Lowe, *Conversations with Gaines*, 321.

[43]Vikor Frankl, *Man's Search for Meaning* (New York: Pocket Books, 1963) 106.

[44]Gaines, *A Lesson before Dying*, 91.

the good community, as we learn to love rightly the other and to practice the virtues that temper the self. Friendship also leads to justice.[45] In the Jesus movement, friendship was the sign of community and of equality. In the Gospel of John, for example, Jesus says, "This is my commandment, That you love one another, as I have loved you. Greater love has no man than this, that a man lay down his life for his friends. You are my friends.... No longer do I call you servants; for the servant does not know what his master is doing: but I have called you friends; for all that I have heard from my Father I have made known to you" (John 15:12–15 RSV). Friendship moves beyond slave and free, male and female, Jew and Gentile (Galatians 3:28 RSV), beyond difference, to community that can acknowledge difference and still express love.

Jefferson experiences friendship and love. Sadly, in a short time, Jefferson experiences all forms of love that most human beings develop over a lifetime: he receives maternal love from his nannan (his godmother), Miss Emma, and even the taste of sexual love from Vivian.[46] This love is connective and compassionate. He also has friends. Grant becomes his friend. He records visits from the children and from old people. He also gains the capacity to judge as an equal, which in the Aristotelian sense, is to treat others as friends. He is transformed from being a victim of the system to one who can look into the hearts of his oppressors as equals and as individuals and know them. Karen Carmean explains: "Jefferson's spelling of 'human' as 'youman' emphasizes his kinship to all members of the community, including his jailers."[47] In this kinship, he gains the right and courage to speak: "Paul trying to be hod when he aint like dont

---

[45]Aristotle, *Nicomachean Ethics*, trans. Martin Ostwald (New York: Macmillan, 1962).

[46]Gaines, *A Lesson before Dying*, 232.

[47]Carmean, *Ernest J. Gaines: A Critical Companion*, 121.

want get too close to me no mo and all the time he is the only one rond yer kno how to talk like a youman to people ikno you paul and i kno old lark and i kno you too shf guiry and you mr picho and mr mogan an all th rest of yall i jus never say non o this befor but i kno yall ever las one of yall."[48] Even the oppressing agents of that structure demand a place in Jefferson's diary, as Mr. Pichot gives Jefferson his pocketknife and, most important, as Sheriff Guidry comes to Jefferson and demands to be remembered as part of this new structure, as good. He demands of Jefferson that he record his fair treatment: "an he say good put that down in yo tablet i tret you good all the time you been yer."[49] Finally, Jefferson can judge the self with love. He hears his own heart. He knows himself: that he had no business being there with Brother and Bear. We see his change as he, when asked what he wants for dinner, does not ask for the gallon of ice cream he said earlier that he wanted, but "just a little ice crme in a cup."[50] As Jeffrey Folks tells us, "The meal is not merely for sustenance but to embody in the ritual a certain image of human existence—in this case the choice to restrain animal impulses and to share a meal with dignity—an act, which to use the language of the novel, separates 'man' from 'hog'...Jefferson's final meal is dignified, not the gorging he had envisioned."[51]

As Jefferson changes, he also redefines the myths that bind and dehumanize him and writes himself, meaningfully, into mythic language. Myth is no longer "an old lie that people believe in,"[52] as Grant tells Jefferson. The "old lie" is the myth of white supremacy. That Jefferson's diary restores myth, as the vehicle of rite of passage to maturity, to full identity, and to

---

[48]Gaines, *A Lesson before Dying*, 230.
[49]Ibid., 233.
[50]Ibid., 232.
[51]Folks, "Communal Responsibility," 269.
[52]Gaines, *A Lesson before Dying*, 192.

belonging community, is symbolized through the image of the door. Jefferson dreams of walking to a door; this is an image that haunts his waking life as well. He does not know what it means: " i dont know what back o ther if its wher they gon put that cher or if it spose to mean def or the grave or heaven."[53] The door is an image of death, of what the afterlife might be, and it is an image of passage, of crossing a threshold to a new state of being. Jesus is also symbolized as a door: the passageway to God. In John 10:9, " I am the door; if any one enters by me, he will be saved." In the Sermon on the Mount, Jesus says, "to him who knocks it will be opened" (Mathew 7:8), indicating that those who ask of God in prayer shall receive. The door indicates approaching a threshold, a transition from one state of being to another. These images of transformation and of salvation and wholeness are confirmed in the last sections of the diary.

In its final stages, the diary becomes poetic. The movement of Jefferson's language to something like verse—like a spiritual—signals that Jefferson is free. He has written himself into being, and like many of the apostles, he has gone out of the prison—not physically, but spiritually. The final images are the moon, the leaves on the tree, a water boy on a cart, and a man in a chair. These images are not focused on or in the cell. The moon and the tree are outside the cell, as if Jefferson has moved outside. These images remind one of the freeing of the apostles from prison. For example, in Acts 12, Peter is bound in prison, and an angel comes and sets him free. Peter "did not know that what was done by the angel was real, but thought he was seeing a vision" (Acts 12:9 RSV). We began by arguing that faith is vision; that vision is legitimate witness. That is true here. Jefferson, though not physically freed, has transcended the cell. Doing so, he can understand his own self. The images of the

---

[53]Ibid., 228.

water boy and the man are two sides of the same reality. Jefferson understands that he is going to die and that society sentenced him at twelve and at twenty. These are the images of the boundaries of his confinement.

Yet, Jefferson has moved beyond these boundaries. He has resituated himself in nature and in society. Jefferson writes:

day breakin
sun comin up
the bird in the tre soun like a blu bird
sky blu blu mr wiggin

The human is integrated into the natural: the image of the water cart is corrected and balanced by that of the man in the chair. However, neither his oppressive childhood (the water cart) nor his coming death (the chair) is a source of terror. The lines are almost like haiku in their spare quality, and their quality of freedom is like that of the spirituals. The spirituals' theology suggests that the weak will triumph over the strong and powerful because God is on the side of the oppressed. The spirituals make a critique from within the system of oppression (slavery) but from the point of view of a higher realm of spirit,[54] Jefferson's diary, like the spirituals, composes its own "representational history of enslavement"[55] that is resistant and empowering[56] and that is in direct engagement with the systems of oppression.

---

[54]Peter J. Paris, *The Spirituality of African Peoples: The Search for a Common Moral Discourse* (Minneapolis: Fortress Press, 1995) 40, 57.

[55]Cheryl Kirk-Duggan, "African American Spirituals: Confronting and Exorcising Evil through Song," in *A Troubling in My Soul: Womanist Perspectives on Evil and Suffering*, ed. Emilie M. Townes (Maryknoll NY: Orbis Books, 1995) 162.

[56]Kimberly R. Connor, "'Everybody Talking About Heaven Ain't Going There': The Biblical Call for Justice and the Postcolonial Response of the Spirituals," in *SEMIA 75: Postcolonialism and Scripturial Reading*, ed. Laura E. Donaldson (Atlanta: Society of Biblical Literature, 1996) 110.

Jefferson's diary is both within (the place of confinement: the cell) and without (from the point of view of the free self). From this double-consciousness, he makes an act of self-understanding: The boy is the man; there is balance. Gaines says in an interview with John Lowe that the diary is "[Jefferson's] way of speaking of his true self, and he could do that when he was alone."[57] The characteristics of the diary suggest the importance of its placement in the narrative. Its placement is crucial to understanding what happens here; indeed, Gaines himself suggests that the diary is a moment of going out: "I had to have [Jefferson]—the Diary—out of the book."[58] Jefferson's death does not free him: he is already free.

The diary also marks the beginning of Grant's freedom. The final words of the diary are a movement beyond the solitary "I"; they are a call—"mr wiggin"—and they are a call to Grant. Jefferson's words do not remain private, therefore, but reenter the call and response pattern of the spirituals. Gaines says that one purpose of the diary is to make it "clear that [Jefferson] was the savior of Grant, so Grant could save the children."[59] Grant, however, does not know that he is saved, and he feels torn and incapable of response.

Grant's initial response is to de-center the self. He, in the narrative, gives us the responses of the community to Jefferson's execution. Most are names we have never heard before: Sidney DeRogers, Lucy Jarreau, Melvina Jack, Clay Lemon and others. All witness—either by sight or by sound ("But my God, the whole town can hear that thing"[60])—the result of the verdict; no one is allowed to claim innocence, to escape the outcome of the judgment the society makes on Jefferson. In sharing his

---

[57]Lowe, *Conversations with Gaines*, 301.
[58]Ibid., 300.
[59]Ibid., 300.
[60]Gaines, *A Lesson before Dying*, 242.

suffering, each is forced into community. Grant recounts Jefferson's self-control and courtesy as he is prepared for the execution—information he must get from others, probably Paul. Jefferson wills his possessions to others, and he asks about the well-being of others, including the sheriff's wife. Grant's silencing of his own voice allows the voices of others to speak, but it also shows us that, like Paul and through Paul, he becomes a witness. The novel begins, "I was not there, yet I was there."[61] Grant assumes this position again at this point in the narrative. He is not strong and neither is he brave, until Jefferson changes him. His early absence is out of pride, arrogance, and fear; his absence now becomes the sign of Grant as a true teacher and member of community: he is the site of multivocality, the conduit of a community's witness.

Finally, Grant will become the man Aunt Emma and Vivian know he can be. When Grant's own voice returns, the nature images from Jefferson's letter carry over into Grant's troubled meditation. Grant's transformation—as necessary to the success of the narrative as Jefferson's—is delayed. Grant holds himself apart. He will not stand with Jefferson; neither will he kneel with the children; instead, he walks around, holding onto the symbol of his power: his ruler. Early in the novel, he is unwilling to participate in hospitality: he refuses to be part of the community because he sees it as compromising his values. Later, he is willing to give, so why is his transformation delayed?

Grant refuses to receive, and, as we have pointed out, the unwillingness to receive is the inability to commit. Gifts, however, come to him. Grant, in his restlessness, believes belief is for others. Then, as he becomes conscious of the world outside his own mind, he sees miraculous signs: the lily, the butterfly, and the blue sky, and he hears the bird, perhaps the one singing

---

[61]Ibid., 5.

outside Jefferson's window. All these symbols point to regeneration and resurrection. The lily is the Easter flower; it holds the divine essence of life and is a symbol of miraculous regeneration[62] and of natural beauty. In the Sermon on the Mount, Jesus tells his community not to be anxious, for God will care for them. He asks them to "Consider the lilies of the field, how they grow; they neither toil nor spin; yet I tell you, even Solomon in all his glory was not arrayed like one of these" (Matthew 6:28–29 RSV). The butterfly—perhaps a monarch, given its coloring, signaling the real power Grant seeks— represents the psyche or soul and its passage.[63] Human souls become butterflies when they are seeking a new incarnation, as Jefferson's spirit will be incarnated in Grant. Birds represent the reincarnated soul: "one of each Egyptian's seven souls…was depicted as a bird, the *ba*, which could put on feathers and fly out of the tomb."[64] The bird represents this freedom from imprisonment and death.

As Grant receives these signs, his movement parallels Jefferson's. He meditates on his past. Like Jefferson, he thinks of his childhood, of playing rag ball. He wonders where his classmates have gone: some migrated, others died. Grant, like Jefferson, is, at first, restless. He is unsure how to respond in this moment; he wants to "sit there" and he wants to run and forget. Mostly, he wants to cry: "God, what does a person do who knows there is only one more hour to live? I felt like crying, but I refused to cry. No, I would not cry. There were too many more who would end up as he did. I could not cry for all of them, could I?"[65] Grant's uncertainty signals change. Like Jefferson, he, too,

---

[62]Barbara G. Walker, *The Woman's Dictionary of Symbols and Sacred Objects* (New York: Harper and Row, 1998) 428.

[63]Folks, "Communal Responsibility," 267.

[64]Walker, *The Woman's Dictionary*, 396.

[65]Gaines, *A Lesson before Dying*, 249.

can judge himself. He realizes that, unlike Jefferson, he is "not there" because he could not stand.[66] He lacks the courage. His crisis comes to a point as the hour grows nearer. He tries to imagine what Jefferson is doing: looking, lying down, staring, standing, crying, begging, standing. In all these possibilities, Grant tries to find his own correct position: "Why wasn't I there? Why wasn't I standing beside him? Why wasn't my arm around him? Why? Why wasn't I back there with the children? Why wasn't I down on my knees? Why?"[67] Grant answers his own question: he will not believe. Though he says that his faith is in Jefferson, he believes that belief is for others. To be unable to believe is to have no hope and no connection, and that, Grant realizes, is the strongest prison of all: "I know what it means to be a slave. I am a slave."[68]

As Jefferson finds freedom, Grant realizes he is bound. How can this bondage become freedom? He must accept the gift, open himself and receive. What he receives is the letter and the friendship of another. Paul brings him both the letter and friendship.[69] Paul represents, in society if not in his heart, the hierarchical system. He is the white man who represents the corrupt law. He, like Saul who becomes Paul (Acts 9), changes through his witness. That law delivers, as the letter is delivered, not legal justice for Jefferson, but moral justice and for the generations to come through Jefferson and Grant. Paul is the witness: "He was the strongest man in that crowded room, Grant Wiggins. He was, he was.... We all had each other to lean on. When Vincent asked him if he had any last words, he looked at the preacher and said, 'Tell Nannan I walked.' And straight he

---

[66]Ibid., 249.
[67]Ibid., 250.
[68]Ibid., 251.
[69]Auger, "A Lesson about Manhood," 83–84n5.

walked, Grant Wiggins. Straight he walked. I am a witness."[70] To
Paul, who has seen Jefferson's strength, Grant confesses his
weakness. When Paul says that Grant is a "great teacher," Grant
replies that he is not a teacher because to be a teacher requires
belief. Even as Paul confirms that he saw the "transformation,"
Grant asserts that he did not change Jefferson. Grant, who has
wanted power, admits weakness. Maybe, he says, "it was God."[71]

Paul, who has not read the letter, hands it over to Grant.
They hold, though they do not open it, the true testimony, the
testimony that corrects the verdict of the court. Jefferson is no
hog; he is a man, and his self is expressed in this document. Paul
asks if he might know what the document contains. Then, he
offers his hand in friendship and says, "Allow me to be your
friend, Grant Wiggins. I don't ever want to forget this day. I
don't ever want to forget him."[72] Grant accepts the epistle and
he takes Paul's hand. This moment of exchange signals Grant's
coming to maturity. He also accepts Paul's offer to return and
witness to the children about Jefferson's final acts, pointing
towards the ongoing friendship that is suggested in the novel by
the details Grant knows and by the name of the child he fathers.
Just as the New Testament Paul insists that the church is made
up of friends, this fragile new thing is cemented in friendship.
The early church is called "the Jesus movement," and a
movement begins here, in Grant and, the text suggests, through
him, in the world. Jefferson's letter and Paul's hand replace the
ruler, the sign of power, and in this moment of exchange, Grant
is changed.

The final moment completes the change. As Grant enters
the true church, the school, the children, whom Grant has
brutalized, whom he has seen as unable to stand, rise, "with their

---

[70]Gaines, *A Lesson before Dying*, 253–54.
[71]Ibid., 254.
[72]Ibid., 255.

shoulders back." As they stand, Grant symbolically kneels: " I went up to the desk and turned to face them. I was crying."[73]

Herman Beavers asks "Who is he crying for? Himself? The children in his class? Jefferson? Are his tears indicative of loss? Joy? Relief? Adulation?"[74] Our answer is, yes. Grant cries in strength and in helplessness, in joy and sorrow. He faces a paradox: he could not save Jefferson, but, according to Paul, he did; he is not up to the task before him, but he must carry on. Grant recognizes that he is not a lone individual, that the community has played a significant role in his creation: "his education...represents the sacrifice of a community," as Beavers reminds us,[75] and Jefferson has died so that he can be free. Now, he can and must take responsibility—pay so that another can go on. This is the dilemma, the necessity and the beauty, of African-American life under oppression. Grant yields, and in this yielding—to his place in community, to his heart, to the children, and to his calling as teacher—in short, to his concrete situatedness—Grant undergoes willingly what he has been forced to undergo in the past—a phrase we will examine in the conclusion. He joins with the community, the least of these. He suffers and he cries, for the past, for Jefferson, for the children before him, and for himself.

"Maybe it was God."[76] With this phrase, Gaines, through Grant, suggests that the process of transformation in *A Lesson before Dying* involves a kairos moment: the human beings and their actions intersect with divine purposes to bring about change in both individuals and in this community—and in us, the readers. Gaines widens the focus of both his characters and the reader. In forcing us into Jefferson's cell and into his mind and soul through

---

[73]Ibid., 256.
[74]Beavers, *Wrestling Angels*, 229–302.
[75]Ibid., 229.
[76]Gaines, *A Lesson before Dying*, 254.

the diary, Gaines lets us experience Jefferson's widening sense of identity as he forces us into the examination of our own identities. Jefferson's final words, "sky blu blu mr wiggin" are images of transcendence and connection. The novel begins with the law of man: with a verdict: a legal judgment. Such judgments move in only one direction: from the powerful to the powerless. This verdict was given long before Jefferson was born. African peoples were made slaves; they were defined as less than human, and they were seen as animals, just as Jefferson is understood to be a hog. Jefferson realizes, before Grant does, what this sentence means: "Yes, I'm youman, Mr. Wiggins. But nobody didn't know that 'fore now. Cuss for nothing. Beat for nothing. Work for nothing. Grinned to get by. Everybody thought that's how it was s'pose to be. You too, Mr. Wiggins."[77] In a sense, the lawyer's cultural pronouncement is more devastating than the sentence of Jefferson's guilt. It, as Herman Beavers explains, maintains racial hierarchy even in the face of the attorney's "fervent and serious" attempt to save Jefferson's life.[78] The discourse does double duty and exhibits the confinement of Southern race and caste more powerfully, perhaps, than any overt violence in the novel. As Philip Auger reminds us, "structures" of white community, in terms of space and of discourse, "are there to disempower, to convict, to imprison, to enslave."[79] Jefferson, therefore, is emblematic of a community in confinement, embodying the sentence for African Americans in a culture of oppression—one that Grant, even with his education and anger, shares.

Gaines shows us how the African-American community defies the verdict, the definition, the ongoing judgment that is not just on Jefferson but on the whole community. Racism is a

---

[77] Ibid., 224.
[78] Beavers, *Wrestling Angels*, 175.
[79] Auger, "A Lesson about Manhood," 77.

destructive myth that has informed the law and that must be confronted daily and changed—though this happens slowly, and, as we see, in unorthodox ways. Within structures of power, however, African Americans are and always have been self-inventing, and writing—the construction of the self on the page is one mode of invention.

The novel ends, not with law, but with what is called "The Great Commandment": to love God with all your heart, mind, and soul and the neighbor as the self. Jefferson comes to love himself and Grant, and his final words place him outside his cell. We have argued that Jefferson writes a "new testament." Christianity understands the Old Testament in light of the New Testament. Paul, in Galatians, emphasizes the shift from law to faith: "Now before faith came, we were confined under the law, kept under restraint until faith should be revealed. So that the law was our custodian until Christ came, that we might be justified by faith. But now that faith has come, we are not longer under a custodian; for in Christ Jesus you are all sons of God through faith" (Gal 3:23–27). Faith is what binds all humanity and embraces, not erases, difference. Faith is paradoxical, and Jefferson's diary is such a site of a discursive paradox or liminality.

Gaines reminds us, using Christian images, that occupying a border is dangerous. It is to confront what a culture holds dear, to challenge the fictions by which it organizes its identity—as Jesus did. Terror—lynching, beatings, rapes, and other tortures—and confinement are tools to keep people from crossing borders and challenging coherence. Jefferson's diary, in its deconstruction of key ideals, both marks them as valuable and appropriates them. For example, Jefferson speaks of the cross,[80] which was a Roman symbol of terror; to die on the cross was to die as a symbol of the transgression of Roman power and to die in humiliation. That

---

[80]Gaines, *A Lesson before Dying*, 224.

which was the sign of terror did not lose that meaning with Jesus' death; that sign became—at the same time—a symbol of salvation. No longer does the sign hold power over a people who are willing to sacrifice the self. The sign of power becomes dialogic and then multivocal through commitment and courage. To develop the capacity to live with(in) this situation of paradox is to be free.

What such language allows us to say is that Gaines is not, necessarily, turning to a Christian vision, in the traditional sense. Gaines, as many critics have pointed out, says that faith is the need for "something higher to believe in."[81] There is, in *A Lesson before Dying*, a reconciliation with religion, with the church—though we do not see as full a reconciliation as does, for example, William R. Nash.[82] As Kimberly R. Connor tells us,

---

[81]Connor, *Imagining Grace*, 151.

[82]William R. Nash, "'You Think a Man Can't Kneel and Stand?': Ernest J. Gaines's Reassessment of Religion as Positive Communal Influence in *A Lesson before Dying*," *Callaloo* 24/1 (Winter 2001) 357–58.

Rev. Ambrose reminds the reader of Ambrose (339–97 CE), who was one of the fathers of the early Christian Church. He was a lawyer and politician, named bishop of Milan by popular acclaim. He transformed his life into one of simplicity and prayer. Ambrose was a friend to Augustine and was instrumental in Augustine's conversion. He translated many of the psalms and introduced Eastern music styles for chanting psalms (Chidester, *Christianity*, 122). He is a doctor of the Church and is the patron saint of chandlers (candlemakers) because "a bright light or halo was seen around Ambrose by his scribe Paulinus while Ambrose was writing a commentary on the Forty-third Psalm. Paulinus described his face as white as snow"; see Michael Freze, SFO, *Patron Saints* (Huntingdon IN: Our Sunday Visitor Publishing Division, 1992) 49. He is also a patron saint of learning.

Gaines suggests, through Rev. Ambrose, named for one of the fathers of the early church, that one institution cannot fully unmake another. The letter does not go to the Church, but to the church as school; it does not go to the preacher but to the teacher, on whom Rev. Ambrose and Jefferson have done their work.

Rev. Ambrose, the symbol of the church in the novel, is powerful, but he is limited. We cannot deny that he aids both Grant and Jefferson. He tells Grant that he lies to bring comfort and to keep going (218), and we recognize those lies as compassionate, necessary, and noble. He is with Jefferson at the

Gaines recognizes the need for traditional faith, but also a need
for a questioning of that faith.[83] How, then, to keep faith and
make change?—the key for Gaines.[84] We spoke earlier of African-
American religious traditions' power to re-appropriate and
redefine. Let us take that a step further to come to understand
what Grant means when he says "maybe it was God" and what
religion might be in this novel.

Historian of religions Charles H. Long, in "Perspective for a
Study of Afro-American Religion in the United States," reminds
us: "To be sure, the imagery of the Bible plays a large role in the
symbolic presentations [of African Americans], but to move from
this fact to any simplistic notion of blacks as slaves or former
slaves converted to Christianity would, I think, miss several
important religious meanings." The Biblical imagery was used
because it was at hand; it was adapted to and invested with the
experience of the slave.[85]

Long goes on to say that African Americans, whose situation
in America is one of crisis, have not interpreted the "inter-
vention of the deity into their community [as] synonymous with
the confirmation of their being within the structures of America."[86] Instead, God has been a transformer of the consciousness
and a resource for maintaining an image of themselves as human
within the definitions of the "majority" culture. God is another
locus of self-assessment. Therefore, internal, not external
structures become the basis for "a new consciousness" for

---

end, but he does not receive the letter. He is with the older generation, those
"who have made a way out of no way" and, doing so, prepared a way for Grant
and the children he teaches. He tells Grant that faith is performance (Beavers,
Wrestling Angels, 177).

[83]Connor, *Imagining Grace*, 151.

[84]Ibid., 152.

[85]Charles H. Long, "Perspective for a Study of Afro-American Religion in
the United States," in *Significations: Signs, Symbols, and Images in the
Interpretation of Religion* (Philadelphia: Fortress Press, 1986) 178.

[86]Ibid., 180.

African Americans. The religious consciousness is the repository of memory and of identity, and God is the transformer of the consciousness.[87]

Transformed consciousness allows us, as we, paraphrasing Long, concluded of Grant, to undergo willingly what we have been forced to undergo in the past. Such rootedness, to use Gaines's term, means that African Americans "freely accept for themselves that which in a previous history they were forced to undergo."[88] Such a consciousness, we want to suggest, is not just a structure of reason—of law. To accept this would be to cooperate with the same Enlightenment structures that enslaved Africans. This consciousness is of the heart—of love. Jefferson and Grant discover love as a balance of reason and power. And, such a consciousness is of the body as well—hence, the emphasis on materiality in the novel: on the human body, on food, and on things—like the radio—that the traditional church cannot see as endowed with spirit. That consciousness in body, mind, and soul is the free space—the human space—from which genuine action can issue.

Ritual action requires structure. In the novel, the prison is the place of the ritual. Within the space of confinement and from the confinement of ritual, an improvisational power is generated. That power is one that meets with the structure from which it comes, changes it, and seeks a new form so that it can generate efficacious action. If God is freedom, action is, finally, "for nothing," as faith is for nothing—it is action that is truly free. Jefferson cannot save the body, but he reveals the depths of the human who is being. "Maybe it was God" necessitates human

---

[87]Ibid., 180.
[88]Ibid., 9.

action, not passive waiting. When the radical freedom of God meets human freedom, the depths of reality are revealed.[89]

It is God as this unspeakable reality, this courageous understanding that Grant experiences. Grant's tears are the evidence of his belief and of his belonging—of things hoped for (Heb 11:1 RSV)—and the evidence of things yet unseen (Heb 11:1 RSV): of his willingness to suffer his own life and the pain of others. Commitment is the foundation of freedom. Freedom, Grant learns, is found only in confined spaces. His tears, therefore, are the sign that he was there, but he was not there—the sign of his fragile, forming, and unorthodox faith.

Works Cited

Aristotle. *Nicomachean Ethics*. Translated by Martin Ostwald. New York: Macmillan Publishing Co., 1962.

Auger, Philip. "A Lesson About Manhood: Appropriating 'The Word' in Ernest Gaines's *A Lesson before Dying*." *Mississippi Quarterly* 52/2 (Spring 1995): 74–85.

Babb, Valeria Melissa. *Ernest Gaines*. Boston: Twayne Publishers, 1991.

Beavers, Herman. *Wrestling Angels into Song: The Fictions of Ernest J. Gaines and James Alan McPherson*. Philadelphia: University of Pennsylvania Press, 1995.

Bhabha, Homi K. *The Location of Culture*. New York: Routledge, 1994.

Caputo, John D. *Deconstruction in a Nutshell: A Conversation with Jacques Derrida*. New York: Fordham University Press, 1997.

---

[89]Gustavo Gutierrez, *On Job: God-Talk and the Suffering of the Innocent*, trans. Matthew J. O'Connell (New York: Orbis Books, 1989) 80.

Carmean, Karen. *Ernest J. Gaines: A Critical Companion*. Westport CT: Greenwood Press, 1998.

Chidester, David. *Christianity: A Global History*. San Francisco: HarperCollins, 2000.

Connor, Kimberly Rae. "'Everybody Talking about Heaven Ain't Going There': The Biblical Call for Justice and the Postcolonial Response of the Spirituals." In *SEMIA 75: Postcolonialism and Scripturial Reading*, edited by Laura E. Donaldson, 107–28. Atlanta: Society of Biblical Literature, 1996.

————. *Imagining Grace: Liberating Theologies in the Slave Narrative Tradition*. Urbana: University of Illinois Press, 2000.

Douglass, Frederick. *Narrative of the Life of Frederick Douglas, An American Slave*. New York: Penguin Books, 1982.

DuBois, W. E. B. *The Souls of Black Folks*. New York: Bantam Books, 1989.

Folks, Jeffrey J. "Communal Responsibility in Ernest J. Gaines's *A Lesson before Dying*." *Mississippi Quarterly* 52/2 (Spring 1999): 259–71.

Frankl, Viktor E. *Man's Search for Meaning*. New York: Pocket Books, 1963.

Freze, Michael, S. F. O. *Patron Saints*. Huntington IN: Our Sunday Visitor Publishing Division, 1992.

Fuller, R. Reese. "Ernest J. Gaines Transcript." www.reesefuller.com/gaines, 6 May 2003.

Gaines, Ernest J. *A Lesson before Dying*. New York: Vintage Books, 1993.

Gaudet, Marcia, and Carl Wooton. *Porch Talk with Ernest Gaines: Conversations on the Writer's Craft*. Baton Rouge: Louisiana State University Press, 1990.

Geertz, Clifford. "Making Experiences, Authoring Selves." In *The Anthropology of Experience*, edited by E. M. Bruner and V.

W. Turner, 373–80. Urbana: University of Illinois Press, 1986.

Gilroy, Paul. *The Black Atlantic: Modernity and Double Consciousness*. Cambridge: Harvard University Press, 1993.

Gutierrez, Gustavo. *On Job: God-Talk and the Suffering of the Innocent*. Translated by Matthew J. O'Connell. New York: Orbis Books, 1989.

Hopkins, Dwight. "Slave Theology in the 'Invisible Institution.'" In *Cut Loose Your Stammering Tongue: Black Theology in the Slave Narratives*, edited by Dwight N. Hopkins and George Cummings, 1–46. Maryknoll NY: Orbis Press, 1998.

Jones, Carolyn M., and John Randolph LeBlanc. "Exploring the Metaphor of Journey." Unpublished paper in possession of author.

———. "Culture, Location, and the Problem of Transitive Identity." Unpublished paper in possession of author.

Jones, Suzanne W. "New Narratives of Southern Manhood: Race, Masculinity, and Closure in Ernest Gaines' Fiction." *Critical Survey* 9/2 (August 1997): 15–42.

Kirk-Duggan, Cheryl A. "African American Spirituals: Confronting and Exorcising Evil through Song." In *A Troubling in My Soul: Womanist Perspectives on Evil and Suffering*, edited by Emilie M. Townes, 150–71. Maryknoll NY: Orbis Books, 1995.

Lepschy, Wolfgang. "A *MELUS* Interview: Ernest J. Gaines." *MELUS* 24/1 (Spring 1999): 197–208.

Long, Charles H. "Perspective for a Study of Afro-American Religion in the United States." In *Significations: Signs, Symbols, and Images in the Interpretation of Religion*. Philadelphia: Fortress Press, 1986.

Lowe, John, editor. *Conversations with Ernest Gaines*. Jackson: University Press of Mississippi, 1995.

Mauss, Marcel. *The Gift: The Form and Reason for Exchange in Archaic Societies*. Translated by W. D. Halls. New York: W. W. Norton, 1990.

Morrison, Toni. *Playing in the Dark: Whiteness and the Literary Imagination*. Cambridge: Harvard University Press, 1992.

Nash, William R. "'You Think a Man Can't Kneel and Stand?' Ernest J. Gaines's Reassessment of Religion as Positive Communal Influence in *A Lesson before Dying*." *Callaloo* 24/1 (Winter 2001): 346–62.

Paris, Peter J. *The Spirituality of African Peoples: The Search for a Common Moral Discourse*. Minneapolis: Fortress Press, 1995.

Thompson, Carlyle V. "From a Hog to a Black Man: Black Male Subjectivity and Ritualistic Lynching in Ernest J. Gaines' *A Lesson Before Dying*." *CLA Journal* 45/3 (March 2002): 279–310.

Walker, Barbara G. *The Woman's Dictionary of Symbols and Sacred Objects*. New York: Harper and Row, 1988.

Doing Time in/as "The Monster": Abject Identity in African-American Prison Literature

Kimberly Drake

What was left was a nineteen year old man lacking the qualities that would have made it human. Now to this man, named Jimmy, each moment was absolute, like a still life photograph. Each happening lived and died, unrelated to the ones that came before or those that came afterwards.... There was no past. No outside world. No thought. No memory. He lived inside a pattern.... It was simply that his mother's visit tipped him into that stunned stage of senselessness which permitted him to do time. In that way it helped, for any old-timer could have told him, you do time on top of each moment, no more, no less, for the past will drive you crazy and the future kill you dead.... *How?* You do not think of it. And *why?* You do not care.[1]

---

[1]Chester Himes, *Yesterday Will Make You Cry* (New York: W. W. Norton, 1998) 69.

So most of these inmates are sick, my friend, but who created the monster in them? They all stand right now as products of their environment.[2]

Chester Himes's most successful novels were those featuring his Harlem detectives Coffin Ed and Gravedigger Jones. His creation of this surreal, violent, and "dark" series of detective novels, however, was the indirect result of the seven years he spent in prison, or rather, as the result of editors' squeamish reactions to the novel he wrote in response to those experiences. Begun in the 1940s, variously titled *Black Sheep*, *The Way It Was*, *Yesterday Will Make You Cry*, *Debt of Time*, and *Solitary*, Himes's first novel was published in 1953 (after six years of revisions) as *Cast the First Stone*.[3] The novel was written in the Richard Wright protest-naturalist style, one of five similarly styled novels Himes wrote between 1945 and 1955. More so than any of the other five, this novel was butchered by editors at Coward McCann, who "deliberately and relentlessly" erased the complexity and "artistic aspects" of the novel to form a "hard-boiled prison novel."[4] Yet it was this "hard-boiled" quality that eventually prompted Marcel Duhamel, the editor of La Serie Noire for Gallimard, to request that Himes try his hand at detective fiction: "start with a bizarre incident, any bizarre incident, and see where it takes you," Duhamel told him, instructing also that he avoid "excessive exposition" and "introspective characters" and focus on the comical, violent actions of Harlemites.[5] The result was a

---

[2]George Jackson, *Soledad Brother* (New York: Coward McCann and Bantam, 1970) 163.

[3]Although Himes's racially oriented protest novels *If He Hollers Let Him Go* (1945) and *Lonely Crusade* (1947) were his first and second published novels, his prison novel was his first novel-length project.

[4]Marc Gerald and Samuel Blumenfeld, eds., "Editors' Note," in Chester Himes, *Yesterday Will Make You Cry* (New York: W. W. Norton, 1998) 9.

[5]Edward Margolies and Michel Fabre, *The Several Lives of Chester Himes* (Jackson: University Press of Mississippi, 1997) 98.

blend of realism, surrealist absurdity, and satirical comedy (*For the Love of Imabelle*) that won Himes the Grand-Prix de la litterature policiere in 1958.

Seen as a series of violent reductions and repressions, the editing of Himes's prison novel provides an appropriate image of prison's impact on Himes. Even a novel about incarceration, it would seem, must suffer in the fashion of the incarcerated; as Jean Genet writes in his introduction to George Jackson's *Soledad Brother*, "any text which reaches us from this infernal place should reach us as though mutilated," although Genet probably didn't mean editorial mutilation.[6] Himes's experience of *Cast the First Stone*'s brutal six-year publication process would have shown him that his literary success depended on shaping his subsequent novels to the audience's taste for pulp featuring racially and economically marginalized characters. To an extent, though, the book's tendencies toward surrealism and naturalism were part of Himes's original text; the uncut version was restored and published in 1998 as *Yesterday Will Make You Cry*, part of Norton's "Old School Books" series. Naturalism allows Himes to explore the ways that social forces and ideologies determine human consciousness. The classic naturalist novel[7] features uneducated working-class characters so constrained by grinding poverty that they have little time for moral decisions or intellectual reflection. Rather, they follow their emotions and instincts, venting frustration at their exhausting struggle for survival with outbursts of emotion and alcohol-fueled violence. It stands to reason, then, that the regulated, surveilled, and otherwise radically determined space of prison will produce characters that, lacking even the distracting necessity of providing food and shelter for themselves, will appear to be

---

[6]Jackson, *Soledad Brother*, 5.
[7]Such naturalist novels were written closer to the turn of the twentieth century by Stephen Crane, Theodore Dreiser, and Frank Norris.

animals, machines, even the "undead." In prison literature, the
standard naturalist character takes on surrealist and gothic
qualities. The characterization of Himes's fictional convicts and
the unstructured plot of his prison novel form a fusion of
naturalism, protest, and surrealism—a kind of blueprint for
subsequent novels, even as his editors' reactions to both the form
and content of *Yesterday* drove him toward the less literary
qualities of this generic mode.

Despite its frustrating origins, this mode served Himes well
not only for his prison novel but also for his protest and detective
novels, enabling him to depict characters who range from violent
inmates and desperately impoverished workers to intelligent and
sensitive intellectuals. The fact that Himes could use this form
for a variety of novelistic modes reveals a significant aspect of his
beliefs about social oppression and its impact on identity. The
vicious and surreal actions of his incarcerated characters result not
only from prison conditions but also from social oppression,
racism in particular. The fact that *Yesterday* features a white
protagonist does not preclude an understanding of the way racism
impacts identity in Himes's work; this is true not only because
the oppression in his fictionalized prison is coextensive with the
social oppression on the outside, but also because the novel
reveals a commentary on the ways in which aspects of identity,
racial or otherwise, are displaced and erased in prison.[8] In this
article, I trace Himes's testimony, both autobiographical and
fictional, as well as the testimony of other convict authors about
the way the prison "program" replaces an individual's identity

---

[8]In thinking about identity, I recognize that, as Cathy Moses notes,
identity is "not something that is imprinted on passive bodies by monolithic
social structures," but a "reiterative process of relations of identification
between the body and social structures." Moses adds that there is "no stable site
for identity—even bodies are subject to change," something that is readily
apparent in prison literature. Cathy Moses, *Dissenting Fictions: Identity and
Resistance in the Contemporary American Novel* (New York: Garland, 2000) 3.

and narrative of development with a uniform institutional
identity, examining in particular the effects of incarceration on
racial identity.

Developed from the short stories Himes wrote in prison,
Yesterday Will Make You Cry is admittedly "not racially oriented."
Himes states that he "did not write about the lives of blacks in a
white world," but about "crimes and criminals, mostly about the
life in prison."[9] In fact, Himes's protagonist is not black, but
rather "a Mississippi white boy" named Jimmy Monroe. In his
autobiography, Himes notes, "that ought to tell me something,
but I don't know what—but obviously it was the story of my own
prison experiences."[10] Suggesting here that his avoidance of race
is an unconscious denial, Himes elsewhere explains it as a literary
strategy; critics have embraced both explanations. Himes's
biographers Edward Margolies and Michel Fabre argue that while
Himes expressed support for "black militancy and black
separatism" and claimed not to "have any use for white people,"
he never "identified himself with" or wrote about "black culture,
except...that of the black underworld," often preferring "the
company of whites as friends and lovers" and behaving in a
manner that "mirrored the larger white world."[11] This comment
suggests that Himes unconsciously allowed an aversion to or
disgust with black culture and a preference for whites to
determine not only his choice of a white protagonist but also his
depiction of black culture, a conclusion that I don't find to be
supported by his writing. Alternatively, the editors of *Yesterday*
claim somewhat unclearly that Himes's choice to "tell the story
of his life using the voice of a white man" enables him "to draw a
few red herrings across the trail and resolve what appeared at the

---

[9]Chester Himes, *The Quality of Hurt: The Early Years* (New York:
Thunder's Mouth Press, 1971) 65.

[10]Ibid., 117.

[11]Margolies and Fabre, *The Several Lives*, 24.

time as an irrevocable contradiction: being a black man *and* a writer and demonstrating that it is possible for an African American to go beyond ghetto experience."[12] Certainly, Himes transcends social expectations by being a writer, but if the editors mean that using a white protagonist allows Himes to transcend the perceived limitations of writing about race in this first novel, then it's debatable whether a prison novel is much of a departure from a novel about "ghetto experience."

Writing about race, of course, is only limiting to the extent that publishers attempt to control the form and content of the literature. These external limits are strikingly clear in the way that subsequent publishers and readers of Himes's novel read and perceived it. As Melvin Van Peebles notes in his preface to Norton's edition of *Yesterday*, the blurb copy for the Signet 1972 reprint of *Cast the First Stone* begins with "the patronizing 'James Monroe was a cool cat'" and describes the "ruthlessly honest" novel as portraying "a young black's agonizing discovery of his own emotions, his own identity."[13] Clearly the writer of the blurb copy hadn't read much of the novel, but what little s/he had absorbed was revised so as to appeal to mainstream readers' growing interest in the "agony" of oppressed African-American protagonists struggling to "discover" themselves. Himes confirms this in a comment about the various rejections of his prison novel: "American publishers" and "white American readers of novels...are not interested in black writers unless they bleed from white torture. I was beginning to bleed, but I had not bled enough by the time I wrote that book."[14] Rather than a calculated choice to escape the racial focus demanded of him, then, Himes indicates here that at the time of writing *Yesterday*,

---

[12] Himes, *Yesterday*, 8.
[13] Ibid., 20.
[14] Himes, *Quality*, 72–73.

his own experience of racism had not yet begun to drive his writing to the extent that publishers desired.

Ultimately, I would argue that Himes's choice to make Jimmy Monroe white can be traced to his undeveloped racial consciousness during his prison years, the result of unconscious denial and deliberate rebellion against expectations. In his autobiography, Himes accounts for his tormented, erratic behavior during his teenage years by saying that at that point in his life, he "simply hadn't accepted" his "status as a 'nigger,'" indicating, again, both conscious and unconscious unwillingness to accept a marginalized identity, something he came to understand around the time he began working on *Yesterday*.[15] Although some of his prison stories written during his incarceration feature African-American protagonists, many more are explicitly described as white and the race of others is unmarked. In a letter to Carl Van Vechten dated 18 February 1947, Himes reveals his desire—and perhaps his desire for Jimmy Monroe—to "escape" his own racial heritage: "As I look back now I find that much of my retardation as a writer has been due to a subconscious (and conscious and deliberate) desire to escape my past. All mixed up no doubt with the Negro's desire for respectability and such."[16] Himes didn't develop a racial consciousness until after his release from prison, "when society began punishing [him] for being black." By 1942, Himes's writing reveals a racial focus,[17] and he describes his "bitter novel of protest"—*If He Hollers*—as the expression of the "accumulation" of "racial hurts" he experienced in Los Angeles between 1941 and 1945 while trying

---

[15]Ibid., 28.

[16]Chester Himes, "Letter to Carl Van Vechten," 18 February 1947, Himes Papers, box 31, 9/7, New Orleans: Amistad Library, Tulane University.

[17]Margolies and Fabre, *The Several Lives*, 49. According to Margolies and Fabre, Himes wrote an article for *Crisis* calling "for a revolution to fulfill the promises of the Constitution."

to get jobs in private industry.[18] From this point on, his writing and thinking about race and his literary treatment of black culture are both complicated and conscious, as is clear from his description of his detective novel series in a letter to Mrs. Geiger, the editor at New American Library: "my purpose was to demonstrate the absurdity of racism in black behavior as well as white behavior and more than anything else to show…the end product."[19] The "end product" is not flattering; as Himes expresses in a 1948 speech on the "Dilemma of the Negro Novelist"[20] to the predominantly white members of a writer's club at the University of Chicago, the effect of oppression on the human personality can be seen clearly in the Negro's "homicidal mania, lust for white women,…pathetic sense of inferiority, paradoxical anti-Semitism, arrogance, Uncle Tomism, …and…self-hate." Although they themselves might serve as examples of "self-hate," Himes's critical statements here are less a sweeping condemnation of his race than an indictment of white racism and an assessment of the damage done to African Americans' "personalities" by the "corrosive inroads of oppression."[21]

His racially specific descriptions notwithstanding, Himes's focus on absurdity as the "end product" of oppression extends from *Yesterday* to the final novel in his detective series, showing his continuing interest in and understanding of the ways social

---

[18]Himes, *Quality*, 75, 61; Margolies and Fabre, *The Several Lives*, 49. Himes was able to begin writing *If He Hollers* after getting a Rosenwald Foundation grant in 1944; his first plot idea for this novel, "a mystery in which white people are being killed seemingly at random everywhere in Los Angeles," reveals the extent of his anger (Margolies and Fabre, *The Several Lives*, 50–51).

[19]Margolies and Fabre, *The Several Lives*, 153.

[20]Margolies and Fabre, *The Several Lives*, 69. This speech can also be found in *Beyond the Angry Black*, ed. John Williams (New York: Cooper Square Publishers, 1966).

[21]Chester Himes, "The Dilemma of the Negro Novelist," Himes Papers, box 31, 23/8, 3.

forces shape identity. However, one could argue that Himes's abovementioned beliefs about the specific impact of racial oppression on African Americans, to whatever extent they were present in his consciousness during the writing of *Yesterday*, would provide a powerful motive for him to avoid any focus on race in that novel. Any anti-racist author writing in the first half of the twentieth century about racially marginalized characters had to be extremely wary of confirming negative racial stereotypes and thus appearing to authorize further violence toward African Americans. As Himes and other African-American authors have realized, "most readers are incapable of empathizing with or imagining a black man's life. Thus, the Negro author's main dilemma resides in the reactions of his audience, in the intellectual limitations of readers."[22] After the prison novel, Himes attempts to delineate in his fiction the process by which African-American characters are damaged by racism. He explains that the "urge to submit to the pattern prescribed by oppression will be powerful," and that the victim of oppression "hates first his oppressor, and then because he lives in constant fear of this hatred being discovered, …hates himself."[23] As he notes in a discussion of *If He Hollers*, in certain cases "the impact of racial prejudice is so severe as to create a motive" for murder.[24] Here Himes is in agreement with prison authors George Jackson and Angela Davis, whose texts demonstrate clearly both the societal roots of black criminal behavior and the ineffectiveness of incarceration.

As previously stated, however, Himes was not at this point prepared to take on the responsibility of portraying an incarcerated African-American protagonist. I would argue, then, that Jimmy Monroe's whiteness can best be understood as a

---

[22]Margolies and Fabre, *The Several Lives*, 69.
[23]Himes, "Dilemma," 3, 6.
[24]Chester Himes, "Letter to Miss Jay Tower," Himes Papers, box 31, 8/9.

"lack" of racial identity following the contemporary understanding of whiteness as "racelessness." [25] As Timothy Barnett
explains in a summary of cross-disciplinary research, "whiteness
maintains power by presenting itself as unraced individuality as
opposed to a racialized subjectivity that is communally and politically interested."[26] Similarly, AnnLouise Keating has described
whiteness as "the guise" of "'colorless' human nature."[27] By
racially mainstreaming Jimmy, Himes can focus on the individual
experience of incarceration, eliminating or greatly decentering
the issue of race. More important, though, is that his act of
"unracing" his protagonist is a reflection of prison life's erasure
of certain aspects of an inmate's identity, Himes's included.

As a crucial part of survival in prison, an inmate's public
identity is a highly contested space. The inmate struggles—often
against other inmates and the prison program itself—to achieve a
reputation that will stave off violence. In a comment about
publishing his first story in *Esquire* while still in prison in 1934,
Himes notes that being known as "foremost a writer" was his
"salvation" in prison and afterward: "the world can...stone me as
an ex-convict, as a nigger...but...I'm a writer, and no one can take

---

[25]As Aaron Winter contends, up until the civil rights movements of the
1960s and 1970s, whiteness "held a position of universality and invisibility." See
"(Dis)Placement and Visibility: (Re)Writing Whiteness in America," a paper
from the Second Annual Conference of the International Social Theory
Consortium (5 to 7 July 2001) www.sussex.ac.uk/Units/SPT/conferences/
st2001/abstracts/wintera.html. For further discussion of whiteness, see also
Ruth Frankenberg, *White Women, Race Matters: The Social Construction of
Whiteness* (Minneapolis: University of Minnesota Press, 1993); Michelle Fine,
"Witnessing Whiteness," in *Off-White: Readings on Race, Power, and Society,* ed.
Michelle Fine et al. (New York: Routledge, 1997) 57–65; and Joe Kincheloe et
al., eds., *White Reign: Deploying Whiteness in America* (New York: Palgrave
Macmillan, 1998).
[26]Timothy Barnett, "Reading Whiteness in English Studies," *College
English* 63/1 (September 2000) 10.
[27]AnnLouise Keating, "Interrogating 'Whiteness,' (De)constructing
'Race,'" *College English* 57/8 (December 1995) 904–905.

that away." [28] In prison, then, his "nigger" identity is displaced by one describing intelligence and useful skill. Significantly, his racial and ex-convict identities become damaging only in the face of the outside "world's" hatred of those aspects of himself. Displacing his racial identity would thus constitute a survival mechanism for Himes, although to what extent he was able to do so during his own sentence is not clear.[29]

Moreover, Himes's various narratives about his prison experience reveal the ways that incarceration facilitates the displacement of aspects of identity even to the point of erasing memories of itself. As Himes notes in his autobiography's first paragraph,

> I knew that my long prison term had left its scars, I knew that many aspects of prison life had made deep impressions on my subconscious, but now I cannot distinctly recall what they are or should have been. I find it necessary to read what I have written in the past about my prison experiences to recall any part of them. I have almost completely forgotten prison, what it was like and what I was like when I was there. The only impression it left absolutely...is that human beings...will do anything and everything.[30]

---

[28]Himes, *Quality*, 117. Notably, Himes only adopts the "writer" label after the publication of "Crazy in the Stir" in the April 1934 edition of *Esquire*, despite the fact that his first pieces, probably written in 1931, were published in 1932 and 1933 in Negro publications (Margolies and Fabre, *The Several Lives*, 36).

[29]There is evidence that Himes spent time around black convicts, most of whom he considered degraded ("dull-witted, stupid, uneducated, practically illiterate, slightly above animal"); this generalization could reveal a contrasting judgment of the intelligence of white convicts with whom he had interacted (Himes, *Quality*, 64).

[30]Himes, *Quality*, 3. George Jackson experiences a similar nerve-deadening disillusionment: "What is happening to me here, what has happened, what will

His own fictionalized narratives of prison life written during
and after his sentence have come to replace his own memories of
the events.[31] The final sentence alludes to the reason for this
repression, the incredible inhuman violence he witnessed,
suffered, and enacted, violence with such force and velocity that
it allows no time for reflection on its impact.[32] As he describes,
"convicts stabbed, cut, brained, maimed, and killed each other
almost every day for the most nonsensical reasons."[33] The
knowledge that at any moment he could be killed or injured
forced Himes into a constant state of high-level anxiety, one
which, paradoxically, demands the repression of any awareness of
psychological trauma. "I didn't have time to think of my hurt,"
Himes states, adding, "I didn't realize at the time that I was
being hurt."[34] His process of repression begins with his arrest
and interrogation, during which he was hung upside down from
handcuffed ankles and beaten by police: "I had ceased entirely to
think, probably when I was being tortured in the Detective
Bureau...I had sealed my thoughts against all reality, against all
contemplation of anything past, present, or future."[35] Himes

---

happen, can never surprise or upset me again. My nerves have been fractured,
my sensibilities outraged, for the last time" (Jackson, *Soledad Brother*, 83).

[31]It is true that Himes's autobiography largely avoids the details of his
prison years, and those he mentions specifically are similarly described in his
fiction. For example, the autobiography alludes to his memory of a convict
sneaking up on a sleeping inmate and cutting his throat while he slept, as well as
the Easter Monday fire of 1930; both are recalled in *Yesterday*; the fire is also
depicted in "To What Red Hell," published in *Esquire* in 1934 (Himes, *Quality*,
63).

[32]Himes adds to this generalization by alluding to the worst kind of
violence—racialized sexual, and cannibalistic violence: "why should I be
surprised when white men cut out some poor black man's nuts, or when black
men eat the tasty palms of white explorers?" (Himes, *Quality*, 65).

[33]Himes, *Quality*, 63.

[34]Ibid., 65.

[35]Ibid., 59.

realizes, of course, that it's "nonsense, even falsehood, to say that serving seven and a half years in one of the most violent prisons on earth will have no effect on a human being," but his intense focus on survival precluded any kind of self-assessment at the time and thus disabled it later.[36] If imprisonment forces the inmate to close himself off from not only outer referentiality and contemplation but also from memory and time, then Himes's avoidance of racial issues in *Yesterday* can be more easily explained. The development of a racial consciousness requires a historical perspective as well as the ability to reflect on memories across time.

The displacement and suppression of memory and identity is part of the prison "program," a process that can be described as "abjectification," in which an inmate relinquishes subject-status through adaptation, becoming a socially acceptable object. I've borrowed the term abjectification from Judith Butler's description of the way subjectivity is created through the active repudiation of socially unacceptable desires. Butler uses the term "abject" to designate "those 'unlivable'...zones of social life which are nevertheless densely populated by those who do not enjoy the status of the subject, but whose living under the sign of the 'unlivable' is required to circumscribe the domain of the subject."[37] When a subject enters prison, certainly the

---

[36]Ibid., 65.

[37]Judith Butler, *Bodies that Matter: On the Discursive Limits of Sex* (New York: Routledge, 1933) 3. In a footnote, Butler further defines abjection as "literally...to cast off, away, or out and hence," thus presupposing and producing a domain of agency from which it is differentiated. She differentiates this concept from a similar one—the "psychoanalytic notion of *Verwerfung*, translated as 'foreclosure,'" which "produces sociality through a repudiation of a primary signifier which produces an unconscious or, in Lacan's theory, the register of the real"; in contrast, "the notion of abjection designates a degraded or cast out status within the terms of sociality...what is foreclosed or repudiated *within* psychoanalytic terms is precisely what may not reenter the field of the social without threatening psychosis, that is, the dissolution of the subject itself" (243).

"unlivable zone," the most "defining limit of the subject's domain," he or she becomes abjectified, I would argue, and thus begins to lose subjectivity, experiencing what Stanley Cohen and Laurie Taylor call "ontological insecurity," a state in which "one doubts the integrity of self" and fears "turning or being turned from a live person into a dead thing, into a stone, into a robot, ...an *it* without subjectivity."[38] In Foucault's terms, prison is a "machine for altering minds," purporting to create a socially acceptable subjectivity through the "correction" of unacceptable behavior and desires.[39] Since, however, the prison administration considers the most prominent aspects of the convict's identity to *be* abject, the destruction of those aspects threatens his/her most basic sense of self.[40]

In fact, inmates understand abjectification, the process of identification with or submersion in the zone of non-agency, as the implicit goal of the prison program. Published testimony of inmates in Walla Walla reveals a common belief that the "policies of the criminal justice system" are "calculated and deliberate procedures aimed at dehumanization," thus seeing their incarceration as a fight between themselves and the system. "The 'powers,'" one inmate states, "want to break me down and make a mindless robot out of me."[41] As Angela Davis notes in a

---

[38]Laing quoted in Stanley Cohen and Laurie Taylor, *Psychological Survival: The Experience of Long-Term Imprisonment* (New York: Pantheon 1972) 109.

[39]Michel Foucault, *Discipline and Punish: The Birth of the Prison* (New York: Vintage, 1979) 125.

[40]In his prison narrative *In the Belly of the Beast*, Jack Henry Abbott refers to the process of abjectification in vivid terms: "If it were desolation you were facing," he says it would "probably inspire you in some way....But what faces you [in the strip-cell] is a cesspool world of murk and slime; a subterranean world of things that squirm and slide through noxious sewage, piles of shit and vomit and piss....If you are in that cell for weeks that add up to months, you do not ignore all this and live 'with it'; you *enter* it and become a part of it" (Jack Henry Abbott, *In the Belly of the Beast* [New York: Random 1981] 34).

[41]Inez Cardozo-Freeman, *The Joint: Language and Culture in a Maximum Security Prison* Springfield IL: Charles C. Thomas, 1984) 52–54.

May 1971 essay written from the Marin County jail, the "structures of oppression" contradict "even the avowed function of the penal institution," which is rehabilitation. She quotes from the Folsom Prisoners' Manifesto of Demands and Anti-Oppression Platform: "The Program we are submitted to, under the ridiculous title of rehabilitation, is relative to the ancient stupidity of pouring water on the drowning man, in as much as we are treated for our hostilities by our program administrators with their hostility as medication."[42] Thus prison administrators' approach to the concept of rehabilitation, the re-formation of inmates' identities to render them functional members of society, serves to make it a process of destruction that inmates must fight. Inmates' reactions to this form of "rehabilitation" are summarized succinctly by Eldridge Cleaver: "society shows the convict its ass and expects him to kiss it," but "the convict feels like kicking it or putting a bullet in it."[43]

More recent depictions of prison programming confirm the ways that incarceration destroys or displaces rather than reforms crucial aspects of identity. These processes form competing narratives in the HBO series *Oz*, beginning with the opening credits of its first episode. In the first narrative, sketched in the credit sequence, inmates experience prison as a chaotic series of frequently violent events loosely connected by an inevitable movement toward execution (credit sequences are interspersed with shots of an inmate being strapped into the chair and electrocuted) and adaptation (credit sequences are also interspersed with shots of "Oz" being tattooed on an arm). Inmates necessarily move toward literal, physical death or permanent identification with prison and the consequent self-

---

[42]Angela Y. Davis, "Political Prisoners, Prisons, and Black Liberation," in *If They Come for Me in the Morning*, ed. Angela Y. Davis et al. (New York: New American Library, 1971) 37.

[43]Eldridge Cleaver, *Soul on Ice* (New York: Dell, 1968) 31–32.

destruction of subjectivity. The second narrative is from the perspective of prison administrators. In the opening action sequence, we witness a discussion between Leo Glynn, warden of Oswald State Penitentiary ("Oz"), and Tim McManus, administrator of Oz's experimental rehabilitation unit, Emerald City ("Em City"). The idealistic McManus argues against the "recycling" of inmates and for rehabilitation, the inmate's progress toward self-control and eventual re-socialization through discipline and skill-building.[44] McManus's philosophy shows some limited success. When he assigns the violently homophobic Dino Ortolani to work on the AIDS ward, Ortolani "befriends" an AIDS patient. However, for the most part, Em City is a "concentration camp" to inmates, a spatially and structurally reconfigured version of the same dehumanizing prison system. Ortolani explicitly disputes the possibility of rehabilitation in an exchange with McManus, stating that "Even with all your good intentions...we ain't ever gonna change, none of us."[45] He subsequently suffocates the AIDS patient—a mercy killing at the patient's request—and is beaten, strapped down, and sedated by prison administrators (actions that lead indirectly to his own death). What *Oz* reveals, then, is that the narrative of rehabilitation, in which an inmate "evolves" from socially unacceptable object (criminal) to socially acceptable subject (reformed, resocialized ex-con) is the opposite of the narrative that inmates experience and testify about, the narrative of abjectification.

Many narratives of prison life refer explicitly to the initial indoctrination, also called "brainwashing" or "processing," as the start of their struggle to avoid dehumanization, to keep "from being molded completely into a gray-clothed, numbered robot,"

---

[44]"Episode 1: The Routine," *Oz* (HBO series), written by Tom Fontana, directed by Darnell Martin, 1997, 0:03.

[45]"Episode 1: The Routine," *Oz*, 0:39.

as Piri Thomas notes in his novel *Seven Long Times.*[46] Once an
inmate enters "those huge green gates of no hope," writes
Thomas, the "process of breaking [him] down as a thinking
individual" begins.[47] Inmates must adjust not only to the radically
determined, institutionalized, and controlled prison program, but
also to the brutal violence, the "culture of savagery" in which
"social controls" are absent.[48] These two opposing aspects of
prison existence, rigid control and uncontrolled violence, are in
fact interdependent, as George Jackson makes clear when he
describes the prison system as organized "terrorism": a
"frightening, petrifying diffusion of violence and intimidation"
displayed by the "offices of the warden and captain" of Soledad.
Violence is not a "side effect" of institutional control but rather
the means by which that control is maintained. Jackson adds,
"how else could a small group of armed men be expected to hold
and rule another much larger group except through *fear*?"[49]
Under these conditions, rehabilitation is clearly impossible, as
the point of this kind of terrorism is to brutalize and dehumanize
a population into abject submission to authority.

Because new inmates have developed their subjectivities on
the outside, often using representations of incarceration as their
"defining limit," they enter prison not only informed about and
fearful of the horrors that lay within, but also extremely self-
conscious about how they will be affected. Jackson was
"prepared" for incarceration because he and other black men are
"conditioned to accept the inevitability of prison," which
"simply looms as the next phase in a sequence of humiliations."[50]
However, his first experience of imprisonment—the "constant

[46]Dennis Massey, *Doing Time in American Prisons: A Study of Modern Novels*
(New York: Greenwood, 1989) 31.
[47]Ibid., 31–32.
[48]Cardozo-Freeman, *The Joint*, 193.
[49]Jackson, *Soledad Brother*, 27.
[50]Ibid., 9.

bombardment of nonsense" and deadly violence "from all sides," the never-ending "attack from the lunatic fringe"—is deeply devastating. Destroying and disorganizing "the logical processes of the mind," it is "the closest thing to being dead that one is likely to experience in this life."[51] Himes's protagonist Jimmy Monroe experiences a similar "death" of self; his struggle to "process" his new surroundings rationally and emotionally is initially inhibited by his absolute inability to comprehend[52] that he has entered that place of his greatest nightmares. He feels "as if he was someone else standing there...not Jimmy Monroe." Part of Jimmy's alienation and sense of unreality is due to the fact that representations of prison do not match his present perceptions: "real prison was the...prison in his mind...a prison of dark, dank dungeons with moldy bones in rusted chains."[53] In response to this perceptual confusion, his analytic and reflective capacities shut down, causing him to "escape into present tense," or "go automatic."[54] Jimmy's response, like Jackson's, is in fact the one intended by the prison administration: the "death" of the inmate's perspective on self and outside world.

This experience of "death" is part of the central psychological effect of imprisonment, the disintegration of the boundaries between the self and the environment, allowing the abjectification of the inmate. In *Space, Time, and Perversion*, Elizabeth Grosz draws on the work of French sociologist Roger Caillois to construct a similar argument about "mimesis," the collapse of the separations between the ego, the body, and the environment under certain conditions: "the relations between an

---

[51]Ibid., 19–20, 26, 110.

[52]In *A Farewell to Arms*, Ernest Hemingway uses the term "realize" in a similar way, to denote the soldier's comprehension of how horrible war really is and that he is in the middle of it; I would argue that there are great similarities between the experiences of modern warfare and prison.

[53]Himes, *Yesterday*, 25–26.

[54]Ibid., 31.

organism and its environment" can become "blurred and
confused" so that the "environment is not clearly distinct from
the organism but is an active component of its identity."[55] In
this particular psychosis, called "depersonalization by assimilation
to space," sufferers "renounce their rights, as it were, to occupy
a perspectival point, instead abandoning themselves to being
spatially located by/as others," thus also becoming an object for
another's gaze.[56] In prison, where the minimum space
requirement for humans is continually violated, a version of this
condition can be induced as inmates lack the "flight distance"
necessary to feel in control of their bodies. Those with unstable
identities (such as schizophrenics) have described "anything that
happens within their 'flight distance' as taking place literally
inside themselves," revealing that for them, "the boundaries of
the self extend beyond the body."[57] Inmates, too, will fight with
each other when flight distance is intruded upon, or "someone
gets in someone else's face. It is not only a spatial violation but a
temporal one as well, as the men state that anyone who *gets in
your face* is *doing your time for you.*"[58] This notion of an unstable
boundary between external space and internal space is
represented as perhaps the most threatening aspect of
incarceration, but also the most inevitable: as one inmate notes,
"You can't run around here trying to be a normal human
being"—you'll be "stripped."[59]

In Himes's novel, conditions in the zone of abjection
continuously destabilize boundaries between self and
environment, damaging individual identity in the process. Images
of disintegrating boundaries in Himes's fiction typically take the

---

[55]Elizabeth Grosz, *Space, Time, and Perversion: Essays on the Politics of Bodies* (New York: Routledge, 1995) 88.

[56]Ibid., 90.

[57]Cardozo-Freeman, *The Joint*, 82.

[58]Ibid., 81, emphasis original.

[59]Ibid., 193.

form of gruesome physical destruction, represented using the conventions of gothic fiction.[60] Upon his arrival, Jimmy describes himself as "internally mangled": after "ten days in prison," he was "all confused and wounded...deep inside."[61] Thinking about his arrest makes him "feel like vomiting...he felt all ruptured down in his groins."[62] His protective shell has been broken, exposing an internal wound that threatens to ooze out. After he is placed into the impenetrable darkness of the "hole" (the "Corrections cells") for refusing to perform heavy labor with a back injury, his thoughts become "broken and scattered," followed quickly by the hallucinatory disintegration of his body: he feels "his brain begin to crack, his skin begin to burst, his bones begin to snap."[63] As the other convicts fight or succumb to hysteria, Jimmy begins to see "his mind standing just beyond his reach, like a white, weightless skeleton. He had the oddest desire to push it and watch it float away."[64] His only physical response to the darkness and the "locked up ferocity floating all around him" is hysterical laughter, a laughter that becomes its own invasive sensation: "that laugh began growing until he could visualize it crawling about inside of him."[65] This image of his intellect or mind (the skeleton) disengaging from his essential self, and his emotions (the laughter) taking over that self, forecasts his method of adaptation to prison life, in which he suppresses rationality and perspective and allows emotion to dictate his actions.

---

[60]The experience of irrationality and abnormality is the essence of the gothic, yet the use of generic conventions by convict writers allows a displacement of their experience, which is not finally irrational or abnormal in context.

[61]Himes, *Yesterday*, 31.

[62]Ibid., 36.

[63]Ibid., 49, 51.

[64]Ibid., 52.

[65]Ibid., 50.

For inmates, it is not only the destruction of identity that makes the loss of boundaries so threatening, but the possibility of merger with the "abject," especially as embodied in other convicts. This abstract fear finds its most concrete representation in the pervasive threat of rape and homosexuality associated with imprisonment. The series *Oz* confronts this fear early in the first episode by showing the most vulnerable new inmate of Em City, Tobias Beecher, manipulated, raped, and brutalized by the racist Vern Schillinger. Rape in *Oz* is another weapon in the inmates' ongoing struggle for domination, yet its horrifying impact stems from the way it abjectifies its victims. Openly homosexual inmates, particularly cross-dressers, are portrayed and perceived by other inmates as abject. The inmates in Himes's novel, too, feel a violent disgust with the openly gay inmates in their dormitory, taking care to suppress or deny any homosexual desires of their own. Jimmy is no exception. He struggles with a growing desire for another inmate named Lively, characterizing his longing for "that golden-haired punk" as "utterly degenerating in its savage intensity"; his feelings "chur[n] together into a squashy, messy, dirty mess in his mind, like the greenish, stinking scum on top of a stagnant pool."[66] Jimmy's experience of psychological breakdown in prison is, for him, epitomized in his homosexual desire; his repetition of the word "messy" acknowledges the disintegration of boundaries between himself and his degrading environment, represented here by Lively. His description of his feelings as the scum on a stagnant pool reveals that for him, homosexuality is the surface manifestation of a tainted system.

Another version of boundary disintegration can be seen in the violent destruction of the physical body. Images of exposed internal cavities and gushing fluids, repeated throughout Himes's

---

[66] Ibid., 196–97.

Yesterday, are perhaps the most terrifying representations of abjectification. However, they also serve to emphasize the universality of the human body and to minimize racial difference. On one occasion, an African-American convict cuts the throat of another African-American convict, "Badeye," who is asleep. Jimmy hears a "sort of gurgle." Looking through the crowd observing Badeye's death throes, he sees "blood bubbling out of his mouth...like the mouth of a dog gone mad," the blood pouring out and pooling around Badeye until finally "he could hardly be seen."[67] Although Himes acknowledges the race of the two convicts, the focus on internal fluids covering the head of the convict is a reminder that human bodies are the same under the skin. Another gory portrayal of the body's interior also features a "colored" convict. Standing near a window shuffling cards before a poker game, Jimmy observes the man hit by an accidental burst of machine gun fire from outside: "the top of the convict's head flew up into the air. He had been making his bunk, and now, on the white sheet which his hands still held, a gooey mass of brains appeared...his mouth was still grinning...but his eyes were gone and blood was coming out over the edges of his skull, running down into his ears...and his hands...gave [the sheet] one terrible jerk...as he fell between the bunks."[68] Jimmy's response to the horrifying scene of decapitation becomes a classic among his poker comrades: "in an inhuman scream," he says "Keep your goddamned brains off my cards!"[69] The emotions Jimmy feels at seeing a man's head fly apart emerge as an accusation that this man has violated Jimmy's spatial boundaries by allowing his internal body parts to contaminate Jimmy's cards. The visual images, however, again emphasize the universal horror of the body's interior overrunning its exterior.

---

[67]Ibid., 55.
[68]Ibid., 166–67.
[69]Ibid., 167.

Himes's portrayal of the undifferentiated internal body represents the transcendence of identity-based difference; this is most clearly visible during and after Jimmy's experience of a deadly prison fire, an episode based on Himes's own experience of the Ohio State Penitentiary Easter Monday fire of 1930 that killed 330 inmates. Wandering around after the fire is over, Jimmy is unable to "push" away the images of the holocaust, unable to "unhook the whole damn thing" from his mind. As he reviews these scenes of death and agony, "change" comes "into him like a chemical reaction, so rapidly you could see it with the eye," and he reaches the "conclusion that night that everything he had ever seen, or ever done, or had ever dreamed of doing, would in the end betray him. That no matter what you had been, or ever hoped to be, a foot of greenish vomit hanging from your teeth would make you much the same as any other bastard."[70] The universality of the dying or dead body, and the way that a focus on survival can erase skin-deep difference,[71] provides the clearest understanding of this novel's racial ideology.

In other prison narratives, however, the threat of boundary disintegration is one reason inmates organize into warring factions by race, sexuality, and religion. Both George Jackson's *Soledad Brother* and Tom Fontana's *Oz*, for example, depict racial violence as an omnipresent aspect of prison life. Jean Genet's introduction to *Soledad Brother* begins by refuting the "idealistic hope" that prison can "strip its inmates of their wretched social differences" (one of McManus's goals for Em City, incidentally), arguing instead that prison is the place in which the racism

---

[70]Ibid., 153.

[71]Describing his post-prison life at the end of the Depression, Himes describes a similar circumstance in which race is transcended: "on the Writers Project" he says, "I did not feel the racial hurt so much...we were all, black and white, bound into the human family by our desperate struggle for bread" (Himes, *Quality*, 72).

permeating American society "reaches its cruelest pitch."[72] Jackson's book confirms Genet's observations, noting that "overt racism exists unchecked" in Soledad.[73] However, in the ongoing battle for power and survival waged in both Soledad and Em City, racial difference is not the cause of but the conduit for the oppression that inmates face; it is a way for the administration to organize factions of inmates and channel their violence toward each other (rather than toward prison officials). Jackson, for example, indicts the prison program itself for the racist violence he encounters daily: "it is not a case of the pigs trying to stop the many racist attacks; they actively encourage them" because most of the guards are white racists.[74] Furthermore, racial segregation is virtually inescapable, particularly in the maximum security or "adjustment" area of Soledad known as O Wing: If a white prisoner from the general population is placed on O Wing for some infraction, he "will be pressured by the white cons to join their racist brand of politics...if he is predisposed to help black he will be pushed away—by black."[75] Indeed, the guards will occasionally "set up" a convict who "has not been sufficiently racist in his attitudes" to be attacked by the black convicts, thus forcing him to seek the society of whites.[76] Similarly, upon entry into Em City, inmates are forced into their "appropriate" racial group without much choice in the matter; only a few successfully defy racial segregation, such as Augustus Hill, the disabled African-American "narrator," and Ryan O'Reilly, the Irish inmate, who affiliates himself with a number of groups as part of his plan to take over the prison drug business.

---

[72]Jackson, *Soledad Brother*, 3, 4.
[73]Ibid., 24.
[74]Ibid., 24.
[75]Ibid., 26.
[76]Ibid., 25.

Both *Soledad Brother* and *Oz* insist that whites, both inmates and administrators, are the perpetrators of racism; non-white inmates react to white racist violence but don't initiate it, according to Jackson, nor do they regularly use race as a lens through which to judge or relate with other inmates, as do whites. In *Oz*, the first instance of overt racism comes from Vern Schillinger, leader of the Aryan Brotherhood, during the first episode. Schillinger asks Tobias Beecher, his new cellmate and soon-to-be "prag," "you're not a Jew, are you?" This is his way of delineating a racial boundary around Beecher, whom he claims as his property (and marks by carving a swastika onto his ass). Typical of white supremacists, Schillinger's sense of ownership and entitlement is the basis for his racism; this is made clear in episode 2, when, against a backdrop of the American flag behind him, he explains that he is incarcerated because of his "fight to protect my constitutional rights...to protect what's mine" from non-whites.[77] Apart from Schillinger's, the only other explicit discussion of race comes from Kareem Said, the Muslim celebrity who arrives in Em City during the first episode. Claiming he is a political prisoner (as does Schillinger, ironically), Said tells Glynn and McManus that "70% of Oz [inmates] are men of color," so that together, they could "take this prison any time we want to"; he adds, "as of today, I run Oz."[78] Said tirelessly attempts to convert or win the trust of inmates from other racial groups in order to build power. His work to this end damages his health when he suffers first from high blood pressure and then from a heart attack—diseases experienced more frequently in men of color because of racism, he explains to the prison doctor.[79] Said's approach to prison administrators seems designed to create more humane conditions for not only black Muslims but African-

---

[77]"Episode 2: The Routine," *Oz*, 0:05.
[78]"Episode 2: Visits Conjugal and Otherwise," *Oz*, 0:15.
[79]"Episode 4: Capital I," *Oz*, 0:42.

American inmates in general. His receptive behavior toward non-black prisoners indicates that his alliances are political, not simply racial. He is repeatedly frustrated, however, by the racist or otherwise hostile responses he receives from other inmates, including African Americans, responses that seem unlikely to change.

While portraying the apparent permanence of Em City's racial divisions, *Oz* also undercuts them by allowing inmates to bridge (or at least consider bridging) racial boundaries with varying degrees of success. In the first episode, as "Wiseguy" (Italian gang) Dino Ortolani is feeling the emotional stress of incarceration, he is approached by Said, who offers to counsel him. Ortolani appears to want to confide in Said but finally walks off, saying "too bad you're the wrong color."[80] In episode 6, Ryan O'Reilly approaches Simon Adebisi, leader of the Homeboys, with a plan to overcome their racial divide so that they can take over Wiseguy leader Nino Schibetta's drug business, which they do successfully. The final episode of the first season, featuring a violent prison revolt, portrays the formation of cross-racial coalitions that hold up until the end, despite numerous tensions. Though the riot was originally the Muslims' plan after Said is given a pistol by a new guard, it begins instead when two white "punks" fight over a checkers game and attack the guards who try to break up the fight. Once all the guards have been disarmed, Said takes control by shooting his gun into the air, shouting "Now, let's get organized."[81] He quickly forms a council of five inmates, leaders of the various racial groups: Adebisi of the Homeboys, Miguel Alvarez of the Latinos, the versatile O'Reilly, and Scott Ross of the Aryan Brotherhood in the absence of Schillinger (Schibetta, the only remaining Wiseguy in Em City, is incapacitated at the time of the riot). Said assigns each group

---

[80]"Episode 1: The Routine," *Oz*, 0:49.
[81]"Episode 8: A Game of Checkers," *Oz*, 0:11.

an area of the prison to monitor, and he and O'Reilly keep the groups working together, reminding them that fighting is exactly what the prison administration hopes they will do. After McManus trades himself for two wounded guards being held hostage, Said tells him that "even the best prison won't be good enough" to put an end to crime, which is caused by racism, lack of education, poverty, and other social factors. For Said, the riot is an attempt to force society to take responsibility for the damage it has created. "We need better justice, not bigger prisons," he states to McManus, adding, "You want to save this prison, and I want to destroy it."[82] The enemy as defined by Said is not simply the prison administration but the social institutions that force the poor and people of color into lives of crime and then create prisons to hold them. At the end, as the riot police enter the prison with tear gas and bullets, Augustus Hill adds to this analysis with the idea that the inmates are simply attempting to (re)create "home." The inmates' revolt is a protest against the state's increasingly repressive regulation (outlawing smoking and conjugal visits, for example) of their "home," Em City, and thus of their identities.

Resistance to the eradication of identity only rarely takes the form of a full-blown revolt in these and other prison narratives, however. Typically, the convict self-consciously plays his or her own reduction and displacement of self against the prison's institutional programming. Inmates must choose on a daily basis whether to immerse themselves in the "institutional routines" of prison, thus complying with the destruction of their identity and according a "type of legitimacy to the institution," or to resist institutionalization, risking even more brutal restriction and punishment.[83] The end result for either, however, is some degree of dehumanization, as Eldridge Cleaver notes: "the Eldridge who

---

[82]Ibid., 0:47.
[83]Cohen and Taylor, *Psychological Survival*, 104.

came to prison...no longer exists," and "the one I am now is in some ways a stranger to me.... Individuality is not nourished in prison, [e]ither by the officials [o]r by the convicts. It is a deep hole out of which to climb."[84] Here Cleaver reiterates a common description of the effects of incarceration, a gradual thinning of consciousness until one exists on the surface only.[85] Antonio Gramsci similarly describes how, after much suffering and resistance, inmates grow used to "being an object without will or subjective personality" controlled by "the administrative machine."[86] George Jackson provides the most severe portrayal of the end result of adaptation on "Max Row," where the "noise, madness streaming from every throat, frustrated sounds from the bars...the smells, the human waste thrown at us, unwashed bodies, the rotten food" cause white inmates to be "ruined for life" and black inmates to be "broken."[87] In Jackson's diagnosis, African Americans are "so damaged" by their imprisonment that "they will never again be suitable members of any sort of social unit. Everything...that may have escaped the ruinous effects of black colonial existence, anything that may have been redeemable when they first entered the joint—is gone when they leave."[88] Adaptation here is simply complete abjectification, the total loss of identity and, ultimately, humanity.

Attempting to balance their inevitable institutionalization with their desire to preserve something of themselves, inmates frequently choose to do "their time on top of each moment": closing off the prison world from outer referentiality and re-

---

[84]Cleaver, *Soul on Ice*, 28.

[85]This is almost precisely a description of a naturalist character, one who has been psychologically constrained and environmentally determined until s/he lives entirely in the present tense.

[86]Antonio Gramsci, *Gramsci's Prison Letters* (London: Zwan Publications, 1988) 188.

[87]Jackson, *Soledad Brother*, 26, 32.

[88]Ibid., 32.

authoring themselves into narratives of chaotic emotional drama. According to a study published by the American Psychological Association, prison lore states that "thoughts of the outside must be suppressed, and involvemen[t] with spouses or lovers, relatives and friends minimized" in order to prepare one's self for likely abandonment; a convict's "head, to remain clear, must be 'inside,' exclusively concerned with prison coping" to the point of developing "a 'shell' which blunts emotion and minimizes affect."[89] Partly, this need to exist in the present tense is a function of the fact that inmates' former lives are moving on without them, and that they have to "either face the fact that...life was over at the moment of entering the prison, or that...life is that existence which takes place within the prison."[90] This realization that they "have been given someone else's time," "prison time," plunges them "continually and inevitably...into considerations" of the "actual significance of the present moment."[91] Himes's character Jimmy acknowledges this on his first day in prison: "just fifty feet away was freedom, he thought. And it would take him twenty years to make it."[92] It isn't long before Jimmy attempts to junk his past and all such time-related considerations.

Most "freeworlders" perceive time as theirs to "use" or "spend," and involuntary memories of past events can be pleasurable because they break "the grip of time," allowing a person to be free of present circumstances.[93] John Frow's

---

[89]Hans Toch, *Mosaic of Despair: Human Breakdowns in Prison* (Washington, DC: American Psychological Association, 1992) 387.

[90]As noted by Cohen and Taylor, a convict "may be serving life, but [s/he] is not serving 'my life.'" In a study done of lifers, not a single one was completely resigned to dying in prison—all had hope of being freed before they died (Cohen and Taylor, *Psychological Survival*, 93).

[91]Cohen and Taylor, *Psychological Survival*, 89–91.

[92]Himes, *Yesterday*, 36.

[93]Genevieve Lloyd, *Selves and Narrators in Philosophy and Literature* (London/New York: Routledge 1993) 138.

metaphor of time and memory shows why this will not work for inmates, however: "memory, rather than being the repetition of physical traces of the past, is a construction of it under conditions and constraints determined by the present."[94] Any construction of the past within the zone of the abject, then, would inevitably taint the memories, making the present even more painful.[95] As described in the epigraph above, Jimmy Monroe's mother's visit, bringing as it did a flood of memories and emotional associations, overloads his capacity for thought and memory, reducing his experience of prison existence to "sensations," which he represses.[96] In pain and despair, Jimmy occasionally wants to "lose his reason, his balance, his perspective...everything that held him to the semblance of a human being—a convict. He wanted to become a blankness, unrestrained."[97] Jimmy's painful struggle to keep his humanity intact and present in the face of institutional pressures to disperse and disappear manifest in his choice of the "present-tense" coping strategy of displacement from referential and familial relationships and total immersion in the daily dramas of prison life. This strategy, however, recapitulates the abjectification of imprisonment and threatens to end his status as a speaking subject.

Rejecting this coping strategy, George Jackson fights the battle against institutionalization through testimony, the narrative reordering of his experiences. Writing the letters that form his book *Soledad Brother* is Jackson's only hope of holding

---

[94]John Frow, *Time and Commodity Culture: Essays in Cultural Theory and Postmodernity* (Oxford: Clarendon Press, 1997) 228.

[95]On the other hand, writing, which "shares with the experience of involuntary memory this possibility of escape from time," can be pleasurable to the convict (Lloyd, 139). Perhaps this is because it "unifies past and present moments in a way that makes of them an identity—extracting from the past something universal which it can share with the present" (Lloyd, *Selves and Narrators*, 139).

[96]Himes, *Yesterday*, 68.

[97]Ibid., 251.

onto his "last two possessions"—self-respect and "mental liberty."[98] Attempting to "repress" a natural tendency to focus on personal emotion, Jackson works to see himself "in perspective, in true relation with other men"; as he notes, "I have enlarged my vision so that I may be able to think on a basis encompassing all, not just myself...but the world."[99] His reading in African-American history, political theory, and philosophy help him develop a leftist perspective on society that he attempts to transmit to his relatives and friends in his letters, in particular, his belief that the dehumanizing prison program is contiguous with racist, classist social ideologies on the "outside." Jackson spends a number of pages attempting to convince his parents that they have "surrendered" their "self-determination and freedom of thought in tranquilizing conformity" to white social norms; their responses seem to consist of incredulity and fear. "You must listen to me. I've been trying to say something," Jackson writes to his mother, referring to her apparent inability to recognize and accept her son as anything but a convict (her "abject"). At one point, he asks her to avoid concluding, again, "George is no good."[100] However unsatisfying, though, his epistolary dialogue with his parents relocates him in a relationship with both referential and emotional meaning. "I need the unquestioning support and loyalty of my mother, father, brothers, sisters," he writes, so that they can all fight the oppressive social mechanisms that, among other things, sentenced him to life for a $70 robbery. He begs his family to "destroy the barriers placed between us with trust, and with love.... Help me when you can, the only way you can, by trying to understand."[101] With their affirmation of his testimony, Jackson can begin to envision the

---

[98]Jackson, *Soledad Brother*, 46.
[99]Ibid., 37.
[100]Ibid., 48.
[101]Ibid., 49.

"possibility" for "something better," a "refuge where people love and live." He can relocate himself into a hopeful narrative of political progress, one that gives him a reason to "stay alive."[102] Rather than survive using the present-tense strategy of immersion in the daily emotion drama of prison, Jackson develops a critical analysis of society's carceral structures and communicates them to his family on the outside, both of which denaturalize prison boundaries.

Jimmy manages to rediscover some semblance of subjectivity at the end of his time at the prison, when he refuses to hide or end his relationship with Rico. Captain Charlie, always friendly to Jimmy, warns him to keep away from Rico because their intimacy angers the other convicts and will get him fired if he overlooks it. Jimmy is infuriated by this warning, especially since he and Rico spend most of their time typing up and editing Jimmy's stories on Jimmy's bunk. He also sees this as a matter of personal integrity, however: "before I'd let these other convicts beat me now," he states, "I'd die and go to hell."[103] When Captain Charlie charges Rico with "sex perversion," Jimmy insists that he be charged as well, later testifying that the charge is "a lie."[104] Jimmy and Rico are convicted and transferred to separate cells on 5-D, "the company of degenerates."[105] Jimmy realizes that by standing up for his relationship with Rico and by sharing the charges, he has lost any chance of a pardon; however, he realizes that "in his warped and unmoral way," his action has "made him a man." He asks his mother to visit and tells her "that the charge was not true" and asks for her help in getting the charge erased from his record. In stating that the charge is a lie, Jimmy is not denying that he has had a relationship with

---

[102]Ibid., 49.
[103]Himes, *Yesterday*, 355.
[104]Ibid., 358–59.
[105]Ibid., 359.

Rico, moments of which "had given him everything," a relationship for which he "did not have any regrets"; instead, he is denying that he has committed "sex perversion."[106] Jimmy no longer feels anguished and conflicted about his relationship with Rico because it no longer epitomizes his abjectification, but instead reveals his strength of character in the face of overwhelming hostility and disgust for his relationship. Until he's transferred to the prison farm—the next stop on the path to release—Jimmy continues to write stories and to allow Rico to edit them. These stories give them both a psychological release, but they are also narratives of his experience, narratives he hopes will be published.

Through oral and written testimony transmitted among convicts and between convicts and families, inmates reclaim themselves from abjection, from becoming a version of "the monster," reconnecting with their humanity in a painful but revivifying manner. In this way, narrative—"an active response" to the "experience of contingency, randomness, [and] fragmentation,"[107]—gives a human face to time, especially to prison time.

Works Cited

Abbott, Jack Henry. *In the Belly of the Beast*. New York: Random, 1981.

Barnett, Timothy. "Reading Whiteness in English Studies." *College English* 63/1 (September 2000): 9–38.

---

[106]Ibid., 360.
[107]Lloyd, *Selves and Narrators*, 11.

Butler, Judith. *Bodies that Matter: On the Discursive Limits of Sex*. New York: Routledge, 1993.

Cardozo-Freeman, Inez. *The Joint: Language and Culture in a Maximum Security Prison*. Springfield IL: Charles C. Thomas, 1984.

Cleaver, Eldridge. *Soul on Ice*. New York: Dell, 1968.

Cohen, Stanley, and Laurie Taylor. *Psychological Survival: The Experience of Long-Term Imprisonment*. New York: Pantheon, 1972.

Davis, Angela Y. "Political Prisoners, Prisons, and Black Liberation." In *If They Come for Me in the Morning*, edited by Angela Davis et al., 27–43. New York: New American Library, 1971.

Fine, Michelle. "Witnessing Whiteness." In *Off-White: Readings on Race, Power, and Society*, edited by Michelle Fine et al., 57–65. New York: Routledge, 1997.

Fontana, Tom. "Episode 1: The Routine." In *Oz*. Directed by Darnell Martin. 1997.

———. "Episode 2: Visits Conjugal and Otherwise." In *Oz*. Directed by Darnell Martin. 1997

———. "Episode 4: Capital I." In *Oz*. Directed by Darnell Martin. 1997.

———. "Episode 8: A Game of Checkers." In *Oz*. Directed by Darnell Martin. 1997.

Foucault, Michel. *Discipline and Punish: The Birth of the Prison*. New York: Vintage, 1979.

Frankenberg, Ruth. *White Women, Race Matters: The Social Construction of Whiteness*. Minneapolis: University of Minnesota Press, 1993.

Frow, John. *Time and Commodity Culture: Essays in Cultural Theory and Postmodernity*. Oxford: Clarendon Press, 1997.

Gerald, Mark, and Samuel Blumenfeld, editors. "Editors' Note."
    In Chester Himes, *Yesterday Will Make You Cry*. New York:
    W. W. Norton, 1998.
Gramsci, Antonio. *Gramsci's Prison Letters*. London: Zwan
    Publications, 1988.
Grosz, Elizabeth. *Space, Time, and Perversion: Essays on the Politics
    of Bodies*. New York: Routledge, 1995.
Himes, Chester. "The Dilemma of the Negro Novelist." Himes
    Papers, box 31, 23/8. New Orleans: Amistad Library, Tulane
    University.
———. "Letter to Miss Jay Tower." Himes Papers, box 31, 8/9.
    New Orleans: Amistad Library, Tulane University.
———. "Letter to Carl Van Vechten." Himes Papers, box 31,
    9/7. New Orleans: Amistad Library, Tulane University.
———. *If He Hollers Let Him Go*. New York: Doubleday, 1945.
———. *Lonely Crusade*. New York: A.A. Knopf, 1947.
———. *The Quality of Hurt: The Early Years*. New York:
    Thunder's Mouth Press, 1971.
———. *Yesterday Will Make You Cry*. New York: W. W. Norton,
    1998.
Jackson, George. *Soledad Brother*. New York: Coward McCann
    and Bantam, 1970.
Keating, AnnLouise. "Interrogating 'Whiteness,'
    (De)constructing 'Race.'" *College English* 57/8 (December
    1995): 901–18.
Kincheloe, Joe, et al., editors. *White Reign: Deploying Whiteness in
    America*. New York: Palgrave Macmillan, 1998.
Lloyd, Genevieve. *Selves and Narrators in Philosophy and
    Literature*. London/New York: Routledge, 1993.
Margolies, Edward, and Michel Fabre. *The Several Lives of Chester
    Himes*. Jackson: University Press of Mississippi, 1997.
Massey, Dennis. *Doing Time in American Prisons: A Study of
    Modern Novels*. New York: Greenwood, 1989.

Moses, Cathy. *Dissenting Fictions: Identity and Resistance in the Contemporary American Novel*. New York: Garland, 2000.

Toch, Hans. *Mosaic of Despair: Human Breakdowns in Prison*. Washington, DC: American Psychological Association, 1992.

Williams, John, editor. *Beyond the Angry Black*. New York: Cooper Square Publishers, 1966.

Winter, Aaron. "(Dis)Placement and Visibility: (Re)Writing Whiteness in America." Paper from the Second Annual Conference of the International Social Theory Consortium (5–7 July 2001).

Faith's Fickle Covenant:
African-American Captivity Narratives
from the Vietnam War

Jeff Loeb

Predictably, a good deal of the African-American imprisonment literature of the last century emerged from its most tumultuous period—the sixties and early seventies. Names like Malcolm X, Eldridge Cleaver, and Etheridge Knight immediately come to mind when the words black and captivity are linked with this era and its images of prison resistance, social revolt, and the dark night of the captive's soul. And in no small part the romantic appeal of such narratives lies in the clear parallels that can be drawn between them and the suffering of their predecessors from earlier decades—American slaves—thus placing these stories in a rich tradition that includes names like Frederick Douglass and William Wells Brown. Yet, nearly forgotten at this point, thirty-some years distant from that period, are the travails of black prisoners of war in Vietnam. Of the dozens of African-American captives jailed in the Hanoi Hilton and other North Vietnamese prisons, two published memoirs of their experience, and each speaks uniquely to both the person writing and the time itself. Norman A. McDaniel, a downed Air Force officer who was imprisoned from 1966 until 1973, recounts his trials in the 1975 memoir *Yet Another Voice*.[1] James A. Daly, on the other hand, was an enlisted man in the Army who was captured in the South and only later transported to the North. His autobiography, also published in 1975, is titled *Black Prisoner of War*.[2] Together, the two narratives, which are radically different in both form and content, constitute a remarkable re-visioning of the forces that deeply divided American society along both racial and political lines for more than two decades.

McDaniel wrote *Yet Another Voice* within a year of his 1973 release, at a time when the POWs were being lionized as *the* American heroes of the Vietnam War. Unlike Daly's memoir (and indeed most memoirs of the Vietnam War), its initial focus is not on any of the familial or cultural events that preceded the traumatic events. There is no attempt, for instance, to construct a previous self since McDaniel represents his writing self as not only intact and unchanged but also as actually strengthened by his trials. In this, his stance resembles that of Booker T. Washington, who admonished African Americans to regard their trials (slavery, in particular) as a cauldron where their mettle had been formed.[3] Rather, McDaniel begins with the ill-fated flight that results in his capture and transportation to Hanoi by the North Vietnamese, and the bulk of the book is concerned with how he endures his captivity. Only after he recounts his being

---

[1] Norman A. McDaniel, *Yet Another Voice* (New York: Hawthorn, 1975).

[2] James A. Daly and Lee Bergman's *Black Prisoner of War: A Conscientious Objector's Vietnam Memoir* (Lawrence: University Press of Kansas, 2000) was originally published as *A Hero's Welcome: The Conscience of James A. Daly Versus the United States Army*.

[3] William L. Andrews, "The Representation of Slavery and the Rise of Afro-American Literary Realism, 1865–1920," in *African American Autobiography: A Collection of Critical Essays*, ed. William L. Andrews, 81–83 (Englewood Cliffs NJ: Prentice Hall, 1993). Andrews argues that beginning with Booker T. Washington, African-American writers began to represent the experience as not entirely negative, at least in effect, in that it produced strong survivors ready to endure the hardships of rebuilding a nation.

freed after six and a half years does he begin to discuss his family. The emphasis is thus on the trial and its aftermath rather than on any sense of loss.

In addition, McDaniel essentially makes the book a vehicle for an extended discussion of his religious convictions, frequently referring to ways in which he has been sustained by his faith, as well as ways in which the society and family to which he returned have rejected that same faith. For instance, he makes clear one of his intentions in the introduction when he states, "Also discussed are some of the perils that we face as a country for failure to serve God and the responsibilities of those who are trying to lead Christian lives."[4] On the other hand, one of the major features of McDaniel's memoir centers on what he leaves out—any mention whatsoever that he is African American. It is as if he desires to efface totally any sense of racial difference.

Daly's *Black Prisoner of War* is the story of a conscientious objector who finds himself in the Army and Vietnam despite his views, only to be captured and compelled to spend five years as a POW, most of this in the South. Unlike McDaniel, Daly emphasizes his African-American heritage from the very first page—the title of the opening chapter, "Bedford Stuyvesant," in fact immediately signals his race—but, perhaps because of his sensitivity to later-revealed circumstances of his cooperation with his captors and resultant charges brought against him by fellow prisoners, he is also anxious to present himself as a mainstream American who believes in the "system." Thus, the afterword, for instance, stresses that he is now (1975) married, the owner of a laundromat in New Jersey ("the first POW to have been aided by the Small Business Administration"), and "optimistic about his future."[5] Whereas McDaniel's self-representation might be interpreted as a message that race should not be a factor in our

---

[4]McDaniel, *Yet Another Voice*, viii.
[5]Ibid., 267.

summation of his trial, or alternatively, that blacks equal whites in opportunity and ability, Daly seems satisfied to represent himself as having earned a measure of equality through perseverance and reliance on a sustaining moral sensibility.

In fact, it is this ethical component of *Black Prisoner of War* that sets it apart from most other Vietnam narratives in general. At bottom, Daly represents himself as a person who acts at all points within the framework of a moral code intrinsic to his self-identity. It is important to note that this is not a code so rigid that he does not subject it to intense scrutiny, and not one so clear in its details that he is free of doubt and uncertainty. Nor is it one exclusively formed by the dogmas of his church, the Jehovah's Witnesses, although their belief in nonviolence forms one of its bases. Unlike McDaniel, he rarely calls on God to sustain him. Faith in some sort of divine providence, while certainly integral to his maintaining morale throughout his ordeal, is nevertheless secondary to more human-centered ethics such as how one treats other people. Ultimately, Daly's is a personal code, syncretic and somewhat pragmatic, but one against which he tests his every action. It is a code capable of sustaining him in the harshest of circumstances, whether the challenges to it are posed by his North Vietnamese captors or the US Army (which the original subtitle, *The Conscience of James A. Daly versus the United States Army*, would suggest provided the more severe test). In fact, *Black Prisoner of War* is in many ways as much the story of Daly's code as that of the events of his captivity. Read this way, the book may thus be seen as a moral history of his life and times, as well as a survivor's narrative and an important autobiography in the African-American tradition.

Another point of difference between the two memoirs revolves around their relationship to their captors. McDaniel consistently represents them as, at best, indifferent but mostly cruel. Even at that, he rarely personalizes them in any way. For instance, though the Americans had nicknames for their keepers—and often, for that matter, knew their real names—McDaniel only refers to them by the generic "guard." Daly's account, on the other hand, remains perhaps the best view we have of the Vietnamese by an American, prisoner or non-prisoner.[6] Not only does he personalize his captors through the use of their names and nicknames, but he also develops their individual personalities for us. Often he recounts his conversations with them on a variety of subjects, most notably the war itself, the relative value of communism versus religion, and the racial situation in the United States. Thus Daly, unlike McDaniel, is able through these often-extended dialogues with his captors to explore the ramifications of race and its impact on the Vietnam War in important ways.

On a final comparative note, the critical reception of the two stories has been as divergent and revealing as the differences between the texts themselves. Of the two major analyses of captivity narratives of the Vietnam War, one, Elliot Gruner's *Prisoners of Culture*, makes Daly's story central while not even mentioning McDaniel's. The other, Robert C. Doyle's *Voices from Captivity*, does very nearly the opposite, largely due, it seems, to his widely differing rhetorical and ideological approaches. Gruner, for instance, states that it is his intention to "break up what I see as a monologue, the dominant myth of the POW experience in American culture."[7] Thus, in arguing that representations of POWs in both media and entertainment, as well as in the interpretations of their own narratives, have resulted in a sort of higher-level imprisonment of American culture itself, Gruner makes clear that Daly's story, among only a very few other published Vietnam captivity narratives, runs

---

[6]Daly and Bergman, *Black Prisoner of War*, 267.
[7]Elliot Gruner, *Prisoners of Culture: Representing the Vietnam POW* (New Brunswick NJ: Rutgers University Press, 1993) 3.

counter to the grain by daring to leave both author and readers uncertain about the story's final "meaning." Gruner suggests that Daly, in this refusal to seek easy closure, "exhibits in [his] text a gaping wound that corresponds to [his] own aversion to continuing to deal with and foreground [his] own experience."[8] Contrast this with the "dominant" narratives of ex-POWs who were also career military officers like James Stockdale or Jeremiah Denton, who confidently represent themselves as finished, unitary selves in complete control of their stories in order to "appeal more to an American audience that has, however vicariously, experienced the pain and suffering of captivity and now seeks a satisfying resolution to the story"—i.e., a hero or a point.[9]

Doyle, on the other hand, seems intent on recapitulating the paradigm of heroism in the face of adversity that Gruner identifies as a prized commodity in American culture. He refers to Daly but once, and then dismissively, saying that his was the only narrative "written as an apology for religious pacifism," and that "Daley [sic] became a Jehovah's Witness in captivity," an inaccuracy of the first order inasmuch as his prior religious pacifism is the major basis for his stance.[10] On the other hand, Doyle seems willing to receive McDaniel's story uncritically, perhaps because it reaffirms in many ways the values that Gruner identifies as desirable in American captivity narratives—perseverance, certainty, and closure. In fact, Doyle not only quotes McDaniel's account of this six-and-a-half year trial as recorded in his memoir but also in at least one personal interview from fifteen years later, as well as his comments in the oral history *Bloods*, published ten years after the prisoners'

---

[8]Ibid., 3.

[9]Ibid., 47.

[10]Robert C. Doyle, *Voices from Captivity: Interpreting the American POW Narrative* (Lawrence: University Press of Kansas, 1994) 34.

release. Neither of these later accounts is, of course, self-generated and are instead highly mediated and edited for consistency with the respective author's own political position.

McDaniel, a career Air Force officer assigned to an EB66C electronics reconnaissance plane, was captured when he was shot down in 1966 during a mission over North Vietnam. Though slightly wounded upon ejection, he recovered relatively quickly. Unlike some other captured airmen and flight officers, he does not report being tortured in his memoir. Rather his incarceration was marked primarily by general deprivation and the kind of day-to-day mistreatment experienced by the bulk of American POWs in Hanoi, especially after 1968 when the North Vietnamese, by then involved in the Paris Peace Talks, became anxious to appear humane on the world stage and ceased the more onerous types of torture. For the majority of his years in captivity, he was held outside Hanoi, in the so-called "Zoo." His memoir is approximately equally divided between his time in prison and what ensued after his release in 1973. What truly marks it, however, is an extensive recapitulation of his previously held values along with a simultaneous rejection of any notion that the experience of captivity has changed him in any way, no matter what has happened to the rest of the world.

McDaniel, for instance, takes pains to represent himself throughout his captivity, which he calls his "ordeal at the mercy of a cruel enemy," as being sustained by a "deep belief in God and the promises of the Bible."[11] As a result of this sustenance, he feels after his release that his identity has remained stable and unified while "the rest of the world [has] moved on," and that, despite attempts to make him "current" and to "update" him, this admittedly retrograde position is not at all negative.[12] In fact, he feels it is his family and his society that have become

---

[11]McDaniel, *Yet Another Voice*, vii.
[12]Ibid., 86.

aberrant, needing, as he terms it, "correction."[13] Toward this end, he immediately attempts to assert his authority upon his return, first by physically punishing his children, who have become "spoiled" in his absence, and next by regaining "control" over his wife, Carol. Using carefully chosen locutions, McDaniel calls her loyalty to him into question, saying that she had become "confused" and "mistrustful" in his absence, and that she had a "difficult readjustment" following his return, including a "conflict the first night" over her "lack of proper parental discipline."[14] According to McDaniel, because of problems she faced when she suddenly became the sole provider for her family—and he appends several examples, mainly of her making major purchases—she "became a sympathizer of the women's movement," although he carefully notes in seeming partial absolution that "she was not active."[15] Ultimately, McDaniel announces that "the grim experience of my loss also shook Carol's religious foundation, which has still not been fully reseated."[16]

At the end of this examination of his home life and his faith, McDaniel remains in a sort of limbo, unable to honestly express or explore his feelings about his experience. Instead, while recapitulating the notion that identity is an almost totally unchangeable quality, he retreats into a sort of distancing objectivity meant to serve as an affirmation of certainty through narrative closure. It seems clear in the memoir that Carol McDaniel, although badly traumatized by the situation, has made efforts, many of them successful, to survive in spite of the circumstances. She has had the benefit of a "normal" community to assist her in this adaptation, and as a result has gone on with

---

[13]Ibid., 93.
[14]Ibid., 93.
[15]Ibid., 95.
[16]Ibid., 95.

her life, whereas McDaniel, without such benefit, has been arrested at some point during his adult development and is clearly unable to adjust to the post-traumatic situation he faces.

Racial identity, however, underlies the most curious aspect of the memoir, mainly that—with one insignificant exception— McDaniel only mentions it in the final chapter, and even then he does not actually identify himself as being African American. Every other black-authored memoir of the Vietnam War except Colin Powell's emphasizes racial difference as a key component of the writer's experience, whether the purpose is to stress resistance or accommodation.[17] Thus, the absence of any such self-identification would seem to run counter to the prevailing mode of representation among African-American writers of war memoirs, but such a rigorous avoidance of the obvious, although oblique, actually represents the most extreme of reactions to the fact of difference: denial. For instance, even when he describes fellow black prisoner Fred Cherry's homecoming speech, widely recognized as one of the emotional watersheds of POW folklore, McDaniel fails to mention the most obvious aspect of that speech: that Fred Cherry was an African American. Given the general recognition by 1975 of how integral racial distinctions—both among Americans and between Americans and the Vietnamese—had been to the prosecution of the war, the point that Cherry was black came to occupy a major semiotic space in much of the self-justifying propaganda that utilized the POWs so effectively in the late-seventies and eighties.[18] No one

---

[17]See Jeff Loeb, "MIA: African American Autobiography of the Vietnam War," *African American Review* 31/1 (Spring 1997) 105–23.

[18]In an interview with Wallace Terry for *Bloods: An Oral History of the Vietnam War by Black Veterans* (New York: Ballantine, 1985), Cherry stresses his African-American heritage from the very beginning of the piece, concentrating on the many aspects of racial difference that he felt and was made to recognize during his confinement (266–91). Despite the fact that they were cellmates for more than a year, and the fact that Cherry mentions several other prisoners by name, he never refers to McDaniel.

who witnessed Cherry's debarkation as it was shown and reshown hundreds of times on television news and in Vietnam and POW specials failed to note that single salient fact, whatever they later made of it. Yet McDaniel seems deliberately determined *not* to mention it, and by doing so, he thus manages also to avoid speaking about himself in racial terms. In fact, except for the dust jacket, which quite clearly announces McDaniel's African-American identity with pictures of him (and which many library copies would not have), the book very nearly completely effaces the fact of his race, and, reading the narrative, one gets the strangest sense of apprehension while wondering when he will give the slightest textual hint of his heritage.

When McDaniel does finally consider matters of race, it is either, first, through circumlocutions or, second, in such a totally objective manner that the text effectively disincludes him through language more appropriate to a social-science text than a memoir. An instance involving both of these attributes follows, one incidentally containing the first mention of racial difference in the entire text:

> In general, I detect an attitude of noninvolvement in most Americans, in some cases due to apathy, in others caused by fear. Such an attitude is most likely due to the residual effects of the discord over the Vietnam war, disillusions and disappointments in the optimistic attempts a few years ago to effect quick changes in our society and government by popular dissent, and the stagnation (in some instances regression) of progress made in recent years toward first-class citizenship in all respects for minority groups.[19]

---

[19]McDaniel, *Yet Another Voice*, 100.

This and the passages that immediately follow, without actually saying so, seem, in fact, to constitute not only a criticism of the efforts of the Civil Rights Movement but also a roundabout questioning of the wisdom of racial change in general. In the succeeding paragraphs, for instance, McDaniel questions the loyalty and motives of anyone who identifies more strongly with any "group" than with the society as a whole—a swipe at the legitimacy of feelings of racial or ethnic identity that came more and more to mark the African-American community in the late sixties and beyond.

Since McDaniel feels repelled and alienated by his family and by the general state of affairs in the United States, he is in effect left with no community, with only his religious faith remaining as a bulwark against the uncertainties that assail him. The result is a retreat into the final voice that we hear from him, which is not that of an individual struggling for self-identity but rather the disinterested social scientist examining—in a revealing choice of topics—the racial situation as it existed in 1975:

> Although in some localities lines of association and cooperation are still drawn on a strictly racial basis, the trend seems to be more and more toward groupings based on "have" versus "have not".... Most black Americans, along with some whites, are disenchanted with the slowdown of progress in recent years toward the full equality for blacks and other minorities in America. The dissatisfactions, resulting mainly from wage differentials, integration efforts, and certain types of employment, are causing ripples but no waves yet.... [W]hether these dissatisfactions will develop into something more serious

will depend on the degree of additional progress toward full equality in the near future for American minorities.[20]

Thus, only obliquely are we made aware of McDaniel's personal racial identity, through a purposeful disinterest so sustained and complete that it constitutes the virtual effacement of that identity and suggests nothing so much as profound denial.

Just as important, by never identifying himself as being African American, he has not only excluded his family but also precluded the immediate possibility of his rejoining that community. Although he has felt sustained by the community of POWs while in Hanoi, and he continues to feel so for a period of time following his return, this community shortly dissolves, for obvious reasons, and is replaced by no other.

If McDaniel is isolated from his community "back in the world," including his own family, James Daly experiences a deep estrangement from his military community, especially those in charge of him. From his opening paragraph, Daly represents himself as operating within his own ethical universe against outside authorities of questionable moral center: "In my senior year in high school, I was still completely convinced I'd never have to serve in the armed forces. That was back in 1966. Of course, I realized that my student classification was certain to be changed after I graduated. Because of my religious beliefs—because I was totally against killing, in any war—I was confident that I would be given conscientious objector status and would not be drafted."[21] It is important to note that Daly at no point contemplates actively resisting lawfully constituted civil authority. Although he never says as much, it is nevertheless clear that such activities as draft evasion are not within the acceptable bounds of his code. Later, after he is in the army, and those same

---

[20]Ibid., 106–107.
[21]Daly and Bergman, *Black Prisoner of War*, 1.

authorities seem to have turned a deaf ear to his entreaties to allow him to leave the service because of his nonviolent beliefs, he on two occasions contemplates illegal acts, first by deserting and second by disobeying orders to report to a new duty station. However, he ultimately decides in both cases, after a great deal of self-searching, that neither action would be ethically correct and thus declines to pursue them further.

Daly's moral ruminations at these points resemble those of white Vietnam survivor-narrator Tim O'Brien, who also contemplates both draft evasion and desertion in his memoir *If I Die in a Combat Zone*, but a major difference is that Daly approaches the decision from the standpoint of a religious conscientious objector whereas O'Brien's quandary, as he readily confesses, is made up of a natural reluctance to put himself in harm's way, coupled with peer pressure to actively resist the draft, as many of his college friends had done. O'Brien reports for duty, serves in Vietnam, and then later recounts the trauma with a great deal of pain and sensitivity in three novels and a memoir. Daly, on the other hand, never abandons his ethical position—while in the army, in Vietnam, or even in his captivity—and his narrative is the ongoing history of and rationale for that decision.

Contrary to McDaniel, who presents nothing of his nonmilitary life or background until very late in his book, Daly carefully constructs a portrait of himself as an industrious, caring, and responsible individual possessed of strongly instilled values. Daly's mother is especially supportive of his achievements in school, his religious beliefs, and his aspirations toward a career as a chef. From the very beginning of the memoir he stresses the support he in return supplies her:

> My mother had mentioned to friends how good I was at doing things around the house, and before I knew it I had

plenty of job offers from families in the neighborhood—cleaning houses, washing windows or cars, and even baking cakes and pies on the weekends. Most weeks I'd end up making only five dollars or so, but that money made it possible to get the things I knew I had no right asking my mother for, things she just couldn't afford. I knew my mother would never do for one what she couldn't do for all.[22]

He thus represents himself as coming from a warm, nurturing family and community. The account in many ways refutes stereotypes (mainly from films) of a uniformly stark ghetto existence. Only in the fact that his father has abandoned the family does it resemble such portraits.

At the same time, the dynamic of conflict over the issue of nonviolence that motivates the entire narrative is set up by Daly's initial strategy of pitting himself against uncaring and unscrupulous authorities. Actually reared as a Baptist, he converts to the Jehovah's Witnesses as a teenager (contrary to Doyle's account, as cited above) but is unable at age eighteen to begin training as a minister, as he had planned, because this would require of him 100 hours a month in community and church service. The demands of his helping to support the family will not permit this investment of time, so he foregoes the training until he can save a sufficient amount of money. To his chagrin, however, he discovers too late—when he receives his draft notice—that not being a minister also means that he cannot legally claim conscientious objector status. In an attempt to discover whether his draft board's decision on this subject is in fact the correct one, Daly (in an act of incredible naïvete) goes to ask his local army recruiter, whom he feels will be more

---

[22]Ibid., 13.

knowledgeable and whom he trusts because the recruiter is an
African American. Naturally, he is duped. The recruiter wins his
confidence, tells him with suitable empathy that the draft board
is indeed correct, and then convinces him to join the service
because doing so will mean that he can choose non-combat duty,
thus providing him a de facto opportunity to live up to his
religious beliefs.

Daly's representations of the problems resulting from his
religious beliefs are inextricably bound up with his perceptions of
racial difference, and in many cases they compound each other.
For instance, his mother, who naturally is extremely upset at his
misguided decision to enlist, counsels him not to reveal his
beliefs about nonviolence to anyone in the Army because she
knows that doing so will only add to his troubles. Daly initially
agrees, reflecting that "being different had always made things a
lot rougher."[23] While thus revealing an early awareness of the
consequences of being classified as racially different, Daly also
seems to suggest, however, through his experience with the black
recruiter, that bonds of race alone are not always sufficient for
trust—that community values and ethical behavior are, in fact,
the correct bases for responsible human relationships.

In addition to being an extended rumination on the complex
relationship between faith and race, Daly's is also a carefully
crafted self-image designed to show both his sense of personal
commitment to his perceived obligations as well as his moral
restraint following his captivity. For example, once in the
service, Daly is immediately made aware of the military's
underlying racism through his white drill instructor: "There were
only two blacks in the platoon, me and another guy. I found out
fast that the sergeant already had us categorized in his mind."[24]
After a series of the sort of trumped-up confrontations typical of

---

[23]Ibid., 9.
[24]Ibid., 11.

boot camp, the sergeant makes it clear that he intends to harass him for the duration, which in fact he does. The experience, coupled with the discovery that the recruiter has lied about his being able to avoid Vietnam, serves to rekindle Daly's resolve to assert his conscientious objector (CO) status in an effort to get a discharge. At each point that he does this—three in all, each at a different temporary training station after he leaves boot camp—he is rebuffed, either by direct denial of his request or by some off-putting subterfuge designed to placate him until he is transferred. Eventually, the Army gives him orders for Vietnam with the terse message that he has been "turned down all the way" on his requests for CO status.[25] Throughout this ordeal, Daly represents himself as patient and long-suffering, following the proper channels and never disobeying orders. Although he clearly sees the connection between his being African American and the failure of his CO requests, he never publicly asserts this linkage. Nor does he condemn in print those officers and NCOs (all white) that deceived and manipulated him, even though it is some nine years later when he writes his narrative, well after the point when any retaliation would be possible.

All of Daly's pre-captivity representations constitute a narrative layer linking his ethical position with his perceptions of racial difference, a sense now expanded however to include not just the white-black distinctions cited above but also those between the whites who are prosecuting the war and their Vietnamese foes. For instance, having been marked as a coward because he refuses to carry a weapon, he is still sent into combat, as well as threatened with prison. Virtually all of the incidents that Daly presents from this pre-captivity period in Vietnam are designed to show the cruelty of the Americans and the suffering of the Vietnamese at their hands, a narrative strategy that seems

---

[25]Ibid., 35.

designed to underscore the essential rightness of his position, as well as the innate racism underlying the war's prosecution. Daly intersperses his descriptions with commentary that makes clear his outrage, while at the same time he castigates himself for not intervening to help the Vietnamese in the various situations described following his wounding and capture.

Because this capture takes place in South Vietnam, and because his captors are not North Vietnamese Army regulars, Daly undergoes trials far different from those of the majority of POWs—McDaniel, for instance—who were, for the most part, captured in North Vietnam after parachuting out of crippled planes. Daly is forced to spend nearly three years being moved from one miserable location to another in order to avoid American troops and bombs, fed only as well as his captors, which is very nearly not at all, and left to doctor his own wounds. Yet, he alone of the several Americans who are in this situation begins to become friendly with some of his captors, carefully humanizing them in his account and in many cases portraying them as morally superior to some of his fellow captives, particularly the white Southerners. In fact, Daly is only able to reenter an American community of any sort when he is eventually transported up the Ho Chi Minh Trail and imprisoned in Hanoi with other POWs.

Daly keeps the examination of his deeply felt ethical sense in the foreground of the narrative during this crucial part of his narrative, along with a growing awareness of the irony of his position as a black prisoner in what amounts to a racist war. He is immediately subjected, like all the other POWs, to continuous indoctrination by his North Vietnamese captors in an effort to break down not only the fledgling community of prisoners but also to gain some propaganda edge in the war of words being fought before the entire world. For instance, they attempt to force several of the Americans to sign a letter condemning the war. Although many do so, Daly initially refuses, feeling that, whatever his personal position in regard to war, his sworn allegiance to his country takes precedence, and that the ultimate consequences of signing would be worse for him because he was African American and a CO: "In the eyes of the army I was a problem...[and] this would mean that the military would single me out for discipline."[26] Because his captors rightly feel that using Daly's race would prove to be an especially effective propaganda tool for them, they also put a great deal of pressure on the other cooperating prisoners in order to get them to help force him to sign. However, even segregating him with other black prisoners and then lecturing the group on the racial inequities in the United States does not convince him:

> But I considered even then how all this was a way of thinking I'd seriously have to question sooner or later. Here I was, truly against the war and everything it represented, probably with stronger convictions than any other POW at the camp—yet I was refusing to sign a letter protesting it. And what really bothered me was that somewhere along the line I had allowed the system to intimidate me. Somehow, I had been made to act contrary to what I believed in—just like when I joined the army and came to Vietnam in the first place.[27]

At length, Daly's doubts extend not just to whether to sign the letter but also to his affiliation with his previous faith, heretofore a sustaining element for him. Ultimately, he decides that the human supersedes the divine, and finally, by relenting and signing, "converts," as it were, to the communist ideology. The basis for this conversion is his dawning sense that

---

[26]Ibid., 124.
[27]Ibid., 124–25.

communism is an activist-based belief, grounded in a desire for human betterment, whereas the Jehovah's Witnesses counsel noninvolvement in their contemplation of rewards in the hereafter. He is "helped" in all this by a particularly sensitive and astute guard/teacher, Mr. Bad (all of the Vietnamese were given such names by the prisoners, based mainly on physical or behavioral characteristics), who counsels him on a daily basis, and after witnessing or hearing about a number of American atrocities—including the poison spraying of North Vietnamese rice paddies and Henry Kissinger's public pronouncements of sincerity and piety while Richard Nixon was secretly authorizing the bombing of civilians.

Daly's lengthy representation of the scope of his pondering and the importance of his decision allow him to present a dialogue of ethics, not just with his captors but also with himself. This dialogue, covering seventy pages (approximately one-fourth of the book), includes discussion of nearly all aspects of the war as well as social and cultural conditions in the United States.[28] When Daly ultimately makes his conversion decision, it is based largely on his reactions to the facts of racial and social difference in America, a point toward which the argument has been building:

> I could understand why the guys in Hark's room [all white and hostile to Daly after his decision] were down on communism. Everything in their backgrounds and upbringing acted to make them resist what Cheese and Roly-Poly [guards] taught. And, of course, the Vietnamese were not able to appeal to them on the basis of [their] being poor and black. That was a hard combination to beat when it came to hard times and hard living in the United States. And the funny part of it was, as much as our

---

[28]Ibid., 133–203.

backgrounds, as Negroes, might have made it easier to be sympathetic to the Vietnamese at times, I sensed, as I often had, an understanding and sympathy for us on their part. Maybe that awareness helped play a role in my going like I did.[29]

This passage not only illustrates the affinity between the Vietnamese and black Americans based on their mutual perception of being classified as racially other by white Americans—an observation made, incidentally, by every other African-American memoirist of the war except McDaniel and Colin Powell—but its tone, one of understanding rather than venom, exemplifies Daly's ultimate purpose in the narrative: a self-reconstruction as one committed to overcoming boundaries through interracial cooperation and assimilation. For instance, while Daly seems to pattern the narrative history of his prison conversion on that of Malcolm X, whose autobiography he reads while in captivity, his attitude toward whites following this conversion is far different from Malcolm's, who, of course, spends much of the latter half of his book condemning them.[30] It might be noted that *Black Prisoner of War* also bears a certain resemblance to early African-American religious conversion narratives—such as those of Zilpha Elaw and Jarena Lee—not only in the sense of the narrator's having been changed but also by virtue of the general attitude of forgiveness toward whites.

The effect of Daly's narrative strategy of representing himself as more forgiving than his white "oppressors" is to underscore the ethical dimension of his character, thereby lending more emphasis to the sincerity of his claims that he is truly opposed to violence. This quality goes directly to the central conflict of the autobiography and is seemingly the primary

[29]Ibid., 180–81.
[30]Ibid., 211.

impetus for Daly's having written it. Indeed, forgiveness and forbearance are themes that he has been developing, although subtly, throughout his narrative, and they are only amplified, by weight of their repetition, after his conversion. For example, never once has he to this point spoken an ill word against the several whites who either failed to process his CO application, in effect condemning him to five years of captivity, or harassed and threatened him for not firing his weapon. Nor does he, later in the book, criticize the actions of the white ex-POWs who bring charges against him after the 1973 Paris Peace Accords are signed and all of them are released and returned to the United States.

Daly is compelled once again, like many earlier African-American narrators, to contemplate just how elusive freedom's nature is, and his notions of freedom undergo a painful dislocation. In effect, his former allies become his enemies, just as his communist captors have previously become his friends. He is kept on a military base, and, while free after a fashion to come and go, he is nevertheless accompanied everywhere by military escorts—black, incidentally, because he is black, thus re-accentuating his sense of racial difference—who are to "assist" him with his transition. His reliance on the absolute defense of ethical behavior is soon proven flawed as a strategy, however, as first one, then another of the former POWs, both officers, file charges against him for treason and mutiny. While both sets of charges are eventually dismissed out of hand by a military court, Daly is now left truly confused and in an untenable position. He is compelled to face the fact that his discharge is inevitable, and he leaves the insecurity of the army for the greater insecurity of civilian life. It is here that the narrative past converges with the writing present, and we are presented with Daly's ending position, one of professed optimism, tinged nevertheless with confusion over the ethics of racial difference.

Daly's closing paragraphs, which identify the writing present as being December 1973, concern both his moral beliefs and the racial situation in the United States, which has changed since his departure in 1967. While still professing to adhere to certain communist tenets, "more and more, I found myself looking toward religion again," he says.[31] His dilemma, which he had first formulated in the Hanoi Hilton, remains whether to be of the world and attempt to change it as well as better himself, or to seek only to spread the word of personal salvation in a distant hereafter. For him, the question turns on his perceptions of racial difference, but the book ends with the conciliatory, assimilative tone integral to his purpose:

> I knew it was going to take a lot to...relive the memories, work through the ideas, to understand. I had returned to a very different society. During the time I was away, blacks had made progress—but I saw this more as a token, ways of pacifying, like the whole Black Capitalism Program, or the gains in politics.... The rioting I remembered in 1965 had quieted, but conditions weren't that much better....Still, I had to find my way in the society I'd come back to. Somehow, to get beyond some low paying job that would force me to live in a ghetto, just getting by, just existing.... I'd have to get busy. Finding a place for myself was going to be a full-time job.[32]

Daly's final comment reflects the spirit that helped sustain him throughout his ordeal: "Maybe in a way I was lucky I went to Vietnam. So many of those who stayed in my neighborhood had

---

[31]Ibid., 265.
[32]Ibid., 264–65.

gotten caught up in crime or hooked on dope. It could have happened to me like that."[33]

Thus, the two African-American captivity narratives of the Vietnam War could not be more different, either in their structure and content or in their rhetorical purpose. While both are stories of deeply religious men, and each is, in a sense, a chronicle of how the writer's faith has sustained him, McDaniel's proceeds from a point of introversion and near-alienation, as if he were a medieval monk retreating into his monastery high on a hill to wait out the onslaught of the pagan hordes besetting his land. Ultimately, he is unable to accommodate himself to the much-changed landscape he returns to, and only his static faith can sustain him in the face of perceived betrayals by his family and his country. Daly, on the other hand, while sometimes as naïve and self-deceiving as any one person could possibly be, nevertheless is able to embrace the changes that have occurred in his world. He also, like McDaniel, relies on his religious faith completely, but, unlike McDaniel, for him doubt becomes strength rather than something to be purged. If in the end he seems more intact than McDaniel, it is, in fact, because he constantly questions, rather than resists, the place of rigid doctrines in a fluid world and thus emerges the more realistic and complete narrator of the signal events in his own life, as well as that of his country in the most trying period of the so-called American century.

---

[33]Ibid., 265.

Works Cited

Andrews, William L. "Richard Wright and the African-American Autobiography Tradition." *Style* 27/2 (Summer 1993): 271–84.
———. "The Representation of Slavery and the Rise of Afro-American Literary Realism, 1865–1920." In *African American Autobiography: A Collection of Critical Essays*, edited by William L. Andrews, 77–89. Englewood Cliffs NJ: Prentice Hall, 1993.

Brown, William Wells. *The Travels of William Wells Brown Including* The Narrative of William Wells Brown, a Fugitive Slave, *and* The American Fugitive in Europe, Sketches of Places and People Abroad. New York: M. Weiner, 1991.

Cleaver, Eldridge. *Soul on Ice*. New York: Houghton Mifflin, 1968.

Daly, James A., and Lee Bergman. *Black Prisoner of War: A Conscientious Objector's Vietnam Memoir*, with an introduction by Jeff Loeb. Lawrence: University Press of Kansas, 2000.

Douglass, Frederick. *Narrative of the Life of Frederick Douglass, An American Slave*. 1845. New York: Penguin, 1982.

Doyle, Robert C. *Voices from Captivity: Interpreting the American POW Narrative*. Lawrence: University Press of Kansas, 1994.

Elaw, Zilpha. "Memoirs of the Life, Religious Experience, Ministerial Travels and Labors of Mrs. Zilphas Elaw." In *Sisters of the Spirit: Three Black Women's Autobiographies of the Nineteenth Century*, edited by William L. Andrews, 49–160. Bloomington: Indiana University Press, 1986.

Gruner, Elliot. *Prisoners of Culture: Representing the Vietnam POW*. New Brunswick NJ: Rutgers University Press, 1993.

Lee, Jarena. "The Life and Religious Experience of Jarena Lee." In *Sisters of the Spirit: Three Black Women's Autobiographies of the*

Nineteenth Century, edited by William L. Andrews, 25–48.
Bloomington: Indiana University Press, 1986.

Loeb, Jeff. "MIA: African American Autobiography of the
Vietnam War." *African American Review* 31/1 (Spring 1997):
105–23.

Knight, Etheridge. *Poems from Prison*. Detroit: Broadside Press,
1968.

Malcolm X. *The Autobiography of Malcolm X*. 1965. Reprint, New
York: Grove, 1966.

McDaniel, Norman A. *Yet Another Voice*. New York: Hawthorn,
1975.

O'Brien, Tim. *If I Die in a Combat Zone, Box Me Up and Ship Me
Home*. New York: Delacorte, 1973.

Terry, Wallace. *Bloods: An Oral History of the Vietnam War by
Black Veterans*. 1984. Reprint, New York: Ballantine, 1985.

Contributors

Tara T. Green is an assistant professor of English and Ethnic Studies at Northern Arizona University where she teaches African-American Literature and African-American Studies. She is the author of articles on Richard Wright, Tina McElroy Ansa, Edwidge Danticat, and August Wilson. She is currently revising her manuscript "A Fatherless Child: African-American Men's Autobiographical Perspectives on Fathering."

Terry Bozeman, who earned his doctorate from the University of Georgia in English, is currently the assistant director of the comprehensive writing program at Spelman College in Atlanta, Georgia. His research interests include African-American barbershop culture; literature, culture, and the American South; and technology and composition. He is currently writing a project on integrating electronic portfolios into service learning courses.

Katherine Daley graduated with her MA in Religion and Literature from the University of Georgia in 2004. She is currently working for the non-profit Council for Spiritual and Ethical Education and is teaching at the University of Georgia.

Kimberly Drake teaches American Literature and Writing at Scripps College. The book project from which her essay is extracted, "Our Backs Against the Wall: The Construction of Subjectivity in the American Protest Novel," is being reviewed for publication, and a new project on social determinism and early twentieth-century American detective novels is underway. Her most recent publications examine novels by Richard Wright, Toni Morrison, and Ann Petry.

Carolyn M. Jones is an associate professor of Religion and African-American Studies at the University of Georgia.

Carol E. Henderson is an associate professor of African-American and American Literature and co-director of the Black Studies program at the University of Delaware, Newark campus. She is the author of *Scarring the Black Body: Race and Representation in African American Literature* (University of Missouri Press, 2002) and the editor of *Go Tell It on the Mountain: Historical and Critical Essays* (Peter Lang, 2006).

Jeff Loeb, who has a Ph.D. from the University of Kansas, is the chair of English at the Pembroke Hill School in Kansas City, Missouri. He was instrumental in the reissue of two Vietnam War autobiographies by African Americans, for which he also wrote new introductions: Terry Whitmore's *Memphis Nam Sweden: The Story of a Black Deserter* (University Press of Mississippi, 1997) and James A. Daly's *Black Prisoner of War: A Conscientious Objector's Vietnam Memoir* (University of Kansas Press, 2000). Loeb has also published more than forty articles in various academic journals. He served in the Marine Corps in Vietnam in 1968 and 1969 as an interpreter and field artillery forward observer.

Dana A. Williams is an associate professor of African-American Literature at Howard University. Her research interests include contemporary African-American fiction and critical race studies. She is the author of *In the Light of Likeness—Transformed: The Literary Art of Leon Forrest* (Ohio State University Press, 2005). She has also co-edited *August Wilson and Black Aesthetics* with Sandra G. Shannon (St. Martin's, 2004).

Selected Index